ALSO BY RUSSELL SHORTO

Gospel Truth: The New Image of Jesus
Emerging from Science and History

SAINTS AND MADMEN

SAINTS AND MADMEN

Psychiatry Opens Its Doors

to Religion

RUSSELL SHORTO

HENRY HOLT AND COMPANY   NEW YORK

Henry Holt and Company, LLC
Publishers since 1866
115 West 18th Street
New York, New York 10011

Henry Holt ® is a registered trademark of
Henry Holt and Company, LLC

Published in Canada by Fitzhenry & Whiteside Ltd.,
195 Allstate Parkway, Markham, Ontario L3R 4T8.

"Psalm IV" from *Collected Poems 1947–1980*
by Allen Ginsberg. Copyright © 1984
by Allen Ginsberg. Reprinted by permission of
HarperCollins Publishers Inc.

Library of Congress Cataloging-in-Publication Data
Shorto, Russell.
Saints and madmen : psychiatry opens its doors to religion /
Russell Shorto.
p.   cm.
Includes index.
ISBN 0-8050-5902-4 (hb : alk. paper)
1. Psychiatry and religion.   2. Psychology—Religious aspects.
3. Mental illness—Religious aspects.   4. Psychiatric emergencies.
5. Peak experiences.   I.   Title.
RC455.4.R4S56   1999
616.89—dc21   98-52122

Henry Holt books are available for special promotions and
premiums. For details contact: Director, Special Markets.

First Edition 1999

Designed by Kate Nichols

Printed in the United States of America
All first editions are printed on acid-free paper. ∞

1   3   5   7   9   10   8   6   4   2

Contents

Acknowledgments

I am grateful, above all, to the psychiatric patients/spiritual explorers who granted me a secondhand experience of the pains and raptures they have been visited with. For those who wanted me to use their real names, I will say a hearty thank you to Joshua Beil, Pam Williams, Jim Byrnes, and Paul Levy. For the rest, I'll fall back on pseudonyms: thank you Margaret W., Marion Davis, Neil Wolf, Andrea, Fay C., Debra D., Barbara S., Charles T., Dorothy, Adam and Ellen, and the others whose stories helped to shape this book.

I am also grateful to the psychiatrists, psychotherapists, pastoral counselors, and other professionals who took the time to help me understand their work, especially Dr. David Lukoff, psychologist at the Saybrook Institute; Dr. Joseph English, chairman of the departments of psychiatry at St. Vincent's Hospital and New York Medical College in New York City and past president of the American Psychiatric Association; Dr.

Francis Lu, clinical professor of psychiatry, the University of California, San Francisco; Dr. Paul Fleischman, psychiatrist in private practice, Amherst, Massachusetts; Dr. Mark Finn, chief psychologist, North Central Bronx Hospital; Dr. David Larson, president of the National Institute for Healthcare Research; Dr. Paul Duckro, director, and Dr. Fredrica Halligan, associate director, Program for Psychology and Religion, St. Louis Behavioral Medicine Institute; Dr. Nancy Kehoe, clinical psychologist, Cambridge, Massachusetts; Kathleen Eilers, chief administrator, and Dr. John Prestby, clinical program director for Day Treatment Programs, Milwaukee County Mental Health Division; Dr. Tim Carson, senior minister, Webster Groves Christian Church, Glendale, Missouri; Dr. Joseph Deltito, lecturer in psycho-pharmacology, Harvard Medical School; Dr. Richard Yensen, director, the Orenda Institute; the Rev. Mike Young, pastor, First Unitarian Church of Honolulu; and the Rev. Andre Papineau, associate professor of pastoral studies, Sacred Heart School of Theology, Franklin, Wisconsin.

I am particularly indebted to Dr. Peter Cohen, psychotherapist in private practice in Princeton, New Jersey, for his profound insights and superb reminiscences, and even more for his bimonthly lecture series "Psychotherapy and the Spirit," at the Cafh Foundation in New York City, which gave me a personal introduction to many people working at this intersection. And I owe a special thanks to Dr. Stacy Davids, clinical psychiatrist in St. Louis, Missouri, who introduced me to this topic.

I also want to thank Anne Edelstein, my agent and friend; William Patrick and Elizabeth Stein, my estimable editors at Holt; and Tim Paulson for his excellent comments on the manuscript. And thank you, Marnie, for everything in the world.

Finally, this book would be paler, thinner, altogether more

anemic if I had not met Anthony Stern, psychiatrist at the Westchester Mobile Crisis Team and longtime lecturer and cogitator on the overlap of psychiatry and spirituality. He opened his library to me; he peppered me with names and telephone numbers of people in the field; he met innumerable blunt queries with gracious, far-ranging, and wise responses, which, time and again, reminded me that the questions in this area are not susceptible to easy answers, but that attempting to answer them is an excellent thing. A few lines of type is tepid payback for all the help he gave, but thank you, Tony.

SAINTS AND MADMEN

1

The New Psychotics

Consider that you are in God, surrounded and encompassed by God, swimming in God.

—MOTHER TERESA

Space is the place.

—SUN RA

The cracking open of Joshua Beil's world began on a thick August day in 1996, in New York's Central Park. Actually, depending on how you figure these things, it could have started at the beginning of that summer. No one knows why a large percentage of what psychiatrists call psychotic episodes occur at the coming-of-age stage of life—late teens to early twenties—but one guess is that the unhinging of one's sense of reality is in these cases related to that first significant severing of connection to home and parents. Going out on your own, planting your identity in new soil, giving it new air to breathe, a chance to grow in new directions, not necessarily the straight-up path your parents encouraged but maybe sidewinding, maybe forgoing the air altogether and burrowing down, exploring the soil itself—such wild freedom may be just too much for some psyches.

In Joshua's case there was an extra dose of disorientation.

He had been born and raised in Honolulu, where body-boarding, pottery, and Bob Marley were his major interests. The only other part of the world he knew was the even more laid-back surf town of Santa Cruz, California, where he had spent his first two years of college at U.C. Santa Cruz. But his father thought he could do with a bit of real-world experience, so he arranged a summer internship at Citibank in New York City. Out of filial duty, Joshua went along with the plan, but the new environment was almost overwhelming; he had never been to the East Coast, and the throbbing, broiling, stiff-necked sky-scraper cauldron of Midtown Manhattan was like another planet. He had no friends in the city, no points of contact with anything he knew, and the pin-striped account jockeys that sur-rounded him might as well have been zoo creatures.

On that day in August, his wandering around the city landed him in Central Park. He was wearing sandals and had cut his foot; he asked someone nearby if he happened to have a bandage. In answer, the fellow handed him a rolling paper. Joshua grinned and said thanks, whereupon the stranger gave him a *shaka*, a waggle of the thumb and little finger, the Hawai-ian "be cool" sign. They began talking; the guy had been to Hawaii. Joshua fell in with the young man, whom we will call Alan, and who turned out to be "temporarily homeless and temporarily unemployed." He had an interesting potential business, though, selling quartz crystals, which he said he had mined himself. He took Joshua to a truck; indeed, the back was filled with crystals. He just needed a little money to get things off the ground. Joshua loaned him two hundred dollars. He was beginning to feel a little light-headed. "Let's go clubbing tonight," Alan said.

They ended up at Wetlands, a downtown club that show-cased world music. Late in the evening, after a few drinks and a modest amount of marijuana, Joshua found himself in a separate room in which a "drumming circle" was taking place. He picked up a drum and joined in. And then it happened. He doesn't know how much time passed, but he began to feel part of the rhythm, that he *was* the rhythm, that he was carrying the whole drumming circle. Very quietly, as if tiptoeing across an unnoticed line, his personality unhinged.

Standing outside the door of his apartment building at four o'clock that morning, he noticed a shadow on the back of his hand. As he watched, it took the form of a falcon. Then the falcon flapped its wings and transformed into a bear, then a bull. He was mildly astonished, and went inside to get a better look at himself. In his apartment, he saw a "rainbow of electrical beams" shooting through his palm. He held his arms out to the sides and watched light pass through his body. He examined his mood, and realized that he felt exhilarated and wonderfully peaceful at the same time. He had enough attachment to reality to understand that something unusual was going on, but he felt sure—and continues to this day to be sure—that he wasn't delusional. "These were not hallucinations," he said, "because I definitely saw them." Instead, he had the strong impression that this was "the beginning of some sort of enlightenment process."

Hold it right there. The glossary of the American Psychiatric Association defines *psychotic* as "grossly impaired in reality testing," meaning that a person loses the ability to tell the difference between the real world and the fairies of the mind. Psychosis involves delusions or hallucinations; one common manifestation of psychosis is "hyperreligious ideation": believing you are God, seeing angels, believing you have a special mission to save humanity. Throughout the past century, and right up to the present, psychiatrists and psychotherapists have done a lot of hand-holding with people in psychotic states, listening to reports of their ecstatic visions, their accounts of meetings with Jesus and Lao-tzu, nodding a great deal, and then beginning the slow job of grounding the person, encouraging a reconnection with ordinary reality by talking about the weather or common objects. There is even a (rather grotesque-sounding) term for it in behavioral psychology: *extinction*; the goal is to extinguish the delusional behavior with a bucket of cold, bracing mundanities. The strategy has been to get the patient out of the state, the way one might climb out of a ditch, and forget about it.

In the days following his drumming circle experience, Joshua found himself submerging more and more frequently into his sublime state of awareness:

> *I might be staring at a tree, and all of a sudden I see the spirit of the tree manifesting itself, the God-createdness of the tree. I see how it relates to the tree next to it, the roots and branches touching the next tree. I see the meaning in that, and it flows over to touch events in my own life, how things that have happened to me are related to other things in the world. People say that everything happens for a reason—suddenly I really believe that. From out of nowhere I'm plunged into moments of spiritual truth and awareness of the interconnectedness of matter and mind and of my place in this beautiful universe— moments of totally feeling the presence of God. I don't need any proof of the existence of God.*

But the bliss soon took on a jagged edge. "Ideas of reference" is a psychiatric term meaning that in a delusional state people often think that other, seemingly unrelated things— song lyrics, TV news commentators—are directed at them. Joshua began "referencing like mad"—he became convinced that radio DJs were communicating coded messages to him; he interpreted casual references to religious figures—the prophet Mohammed, Jah Rastafari—as pointed at him.

Two weeks after the drumming circle experience, Josh's summer was over and he was due back at school in Santa Cruz. In Hawaii his parents had begun to suspect that something was wrong, however, and asked him to come home before he returned to college. Up to this point, Joshua hadn't talked to anyone about what he was experiencing; he was convinced that if he did so people would try to halt his journey to enlightenment. In Honolulu, he did what he called a "red shirt/blue shirt routine" for his parents' benefit: "You know, it's like, you wake up one morning and put on a bright red shirt, and everyone compliments you on your beautiful blue shirt. You're confused so you look in the mirror, but you keep seeing a red shirt. The point of the parable is, what color is the shirt? While I was in Hawaii, I told my parents what they wanted to hear. I said, 'Yeah, it's a blue shirt.' "

Having successfully ducked his parents' fears, he went back to Santa Cruz, where he roamed the beach and wandered in the redwood forests, dumb with wonder and feeling "this intense connectedness with everything around me." He reviewed his past, particularly episodes that had troubled him, and saw them with a new, broader vision. He asked for forgiveness for past wrongs, and felt cleansed.

The semester started, and he found that schoolwork was much more difficult. A single sentence in a homework assignment might arrest him with its cosmic significance, so that he could go no further. He could see the auras of professors; he became convinced that one professor, whose aura appeared as a beam of light coming straight down from the ceiling to engulf her, was an angel. He developed an elaborate angelology: the unseen spaces of the universe were peopled by hosts of good and evil creatures, and they liked to place bets over his smallest actions. The act of putting on shoes became a moral battle, with phalanxes of cosmic creatures casting bets on which shoe would go on first. He would go catatonic, rigid in fear that he might choose the wrong shoe and send the universe out of moral alignment. One way out of the dilemma was to decide not to wear shoes; he frequently opted for this solution.

Things descended quickly. Televisions, telephones, microwave ovens—any electrical device might be bugged or used by one or another angel gang to coerce him. He started to rave. He stopped bathing; for several days he didn't eat, sleep, or change his clothes. He was too far gone to even know who reported him, but on October 22, Santa Cruz police officers came to his dorm room and took him into custody on California Code 5150, being a danger to oneself.

One might think the nightmarish aspect of the experience was over at this point, but in fact it was just beginning. As he was taken away—barefoot, filthy, in ankle restraints and handcuffs—he remained very still and tried to keep his mind from exploring the depths that had become normal: "I felt that anyone of any importance could read my mind. It seemed natural that they were doing this to me. It was Christ-like. It confirmed the delusion that I was important. They were going to crucify me."

If the fact that he had become godlike was now known by his enemies, whose agents were about to torture him and experiment on him, he could at least tell them that he understood their game. At Belmont Hills Psychiatric Hospital in Santa Cruz, psychiatrists administered a standard reality test called Draw a Person; they gave him a piece of paper and a pen, and asked him to draw a human figure. He swiftly drew a clear, recognizable body with all of the major features, then he asked them for a second sheet. With this one he took his time, covering it with circles, eyes, linked infinity symbols, connecting arrows. He handed both sheets to the doctor, leaned in close for emphasis, pointed first at the man and then at the other drawing, and said, "This is what you wanted me to draw. *This is what it is.*" His initiation in the mysteries had progressed too far for him to humor anyone with any more games of red shirt/ blue shirt.

His psychiatrist at Belmont Hills believed he was in an acute manic episode with schizophreniclike symptoms, and that he showed signs of schizoaffective disorder, a combination of schizophrenia and bipolar disorder, a condition from which a large percentage of patients do not recover. She prescribed Haldol, a powerful antipsychotic medication designed to grip the reins of the mind, pull the charging teams of ideas to a halt, and blinker them to prevent any straying. The side effects of Haldol can include, in the words of the *Synopsis of Psychiatry*, "acute dystonic reactions and Parkinsonian symptoms"—neck and tongue spasms, face twitches, and stiffness, as well as "cognitive dulling."[1] At large doses it produces what mental patients refer to as the Haldol Shuffle, a zombie-like walk, eyes down, slippers scraping along linoleum floors, facial features giving the distinct impression that very little is going on upstairs. The psychiatrist also put him on lithium to control his mania and regulate his mood.

Meanwhile, Drake and Judy Beil sat at their son's bedside stricken with anxiety. "It was absolutely frightening to think that we had sent off into the world a gifted kid and what came back was a vegetable," said Drake Beil. "We were overcome by guilt. Did we fail in preparing him to deal with the real world? And through it all was the thought that he might not come back, that this might last forever." The emotional low-point was the day Drake Beil pulled out the same building blocks Joshua had played with as a two-year-old and carefully stacked them up in front of his debilitated son. "I said, 'Let me show you what I think is happening here. These blocks are inside your head. Now, maybe they just got knocked down, in which case we can build them back up.' But . . . maybe they're not there anymore."

But the blocks were still there. Over the next several weeks Joshua was moved from the hospital in California to one in Hawaii, taken off Haldol, and given another, newer antipsychotic drug called Risperdal. His memories of his weeks in various hospitals are classic horror stuff: men in white lab coats coming and going, leaning in to ogle at you; time out of whack; diving into sleep as into a refuge; more lab coats; his parents' faces leaning in, their voices seeming distorted. All of it hazed, as if experienced through cheesecloth.

And then . . . done. Joshua was to be one of the lucky ones: the antipsychotics had done the trick; his consciousness came swimming back to the surface. One day sitting with his parents, *Wheel of Fortune* came on the television. "All of a sudden Josh started guessing the puzzle and goofing on the contestants," his father said. "Then he turned to me and said, 'Josh has entered the building.' "

Joshua was released into his parents' care. He still felt a profound confusion and disorientation, but he knew he was back, that it was over. He could now put the whole ugly episode behind him and begin the slow task of getting on with his life. He took a couple of classes at a community college, got a job at a local Starbucks, made plans to re-enroll in college and finish his degree.

But no, it wasn't going to be that neat. He couldn't just forget. In many respects, Joshua's story is fairly commonplace. Psychosis is a general term that covers a wide variety of out-of-touch-with-reality conditions; one of the most common and severe of these, schizophrenia, afflicts two million Americans, nearly 1 percent of the population. At least 40 percent of those who are laid low by a schizphrenialike episode will develop it as a more or less permanent condition. For those lucky ones who are visited by a single psychotic episode that then vanishes, most, following professional advice, treat it as something akin to a vicious bout of the flu and push ahead with their lives. Joshua's encounter with mental illness entered a different category, a whole new realm, when, after the illness itself, he decided not to let go of it.

Why would he decide such a thing? Because, simply, it had felt good—it had felt wonderful. There was something so wonderful about it, in fact, that it seemed to crack through his ordinary way of knowing himself and the world and deliver him into a new awareness of the world as whole and true, and of himself as an integral part of it. It was so wonderful that the memory of it still glinted through all the horror and murk that had surrounded it. Because of it, Joshua had a glimmer of himself as a better, fuller, healthier person. How could that be bad? Yes, there was a great deal of horror and neurological mayhem involved in the experience, but equally surely there was something so profound and blissful that he simply couldn't let it drift away:

> *I close my eyes and look directly at the sun and feel the warmth. I know it is God, like a form of communication that he uses. Why didn't I know this before? It's so obvious, so obviously HIM. I am blissed-out on the world itself. I understand the internal workings of the universe and my role within it, the innerconnectedness of all things.*

It was this determination to hold on to his psychotic experience that made Joshua different. He was one of what might be called the New Psychotics, people who, even after returning to sanity, continue to believe that their mental illness somehow pushed them into a state of spiritual awareness. Granted, people have done something similar in the past. Anthropologists have studied the ritualization of this state of consciousness in primitive societies: how, at around the time of adolescence, tribal youths undergo a ceremonial form of madness, sometimes involving the use of psychoactive drugs to bring on the altered state. The rite-of-passage ceremony signals the death of childhood and the birth of a new adult member of the community; it is, by some thinking, an institutionalized way to manage what comes about haphazardly in cases such as Joshua's. And while it is impossible to be certain, especially since psychosis is such a modern notion, various people throughout history may have seen themselves as having gone through both a psychotic and a mystical experience. On such a list might be found Saint Paul, Saint Teresa of Avila, Martin Luther, Saint Francis of Assisi, the playwright August Strindberg, George Fox, the founder of Quakerism, the dramatist Antonin Artaud, and the writers Allen Ginsberg and Dostoevsky.

Unlike these famous sufferers, however, Joshua came to his determination at a crucial time in the history of the psychotherapeutic professions. On January 4, 1993, in a meeting of almost surreal historical proportions, Dr. Joseph English, president of the American Psychiatric Association, entered the Vatican Palace and commenced a dialogue about sin, guilt, God, and medicine with Pope John Paul II. These representatives of two world-historic priesthoods did not merely exchange platitudes, but seemed actually to see eye to eye on some fundamental points. Dr. English, the representative of a field that has traditionally treated religion as a form of illness, told the pope, "Some of us feel, in the spirit of this season, that we have followed a star to be with you on this day, that we are here in the spirit of Epiphany." Perhaps more remarkably, after the pope had expressed his belief that a full understanding of an individual must take into account the "spiritual dimension and capacity for self-transcendence," the psychiatrist agreed.

The meeting between the psychiatrist and the pope was reported in news media around the world as a milestone. In fact, it was a metaphoric climax to a quiet but remarkable change of outlook that had been building over the previous decade or so. Everyone knows that psychology speaks a language that is profoundly different from religious language, that the two spring from different eras of human history and involve different understandings not just of human beings but of even vaster enterprises: life, the universe. And many people know of various recent efforts by psychologists to link their field with some religious tradition or technique, such as meditation.

What may not be so well known is just how widespread is this reaching out to religion on the part of psychologists and psychiatrists. These modern sciences of the individual, born in the age of Queen Victoria, are transforming themselves before our eyes. Many professionals in these fields have come so far from Freud's classic definition of religious experience ("regression to primary narcissism") that they believe it is a biological fact of life, that religion is in our genes.

One result of this change of thinking is that there are now mental health professionals who are willing to examine people like Joshua Beil with a widened ontological lens. Some people in the profession want to study psychotic delusions and mystical experiences side by side, to bring religious experience into the realm of science.

As recently as the 1970s, the standard thinking in psychiatry was that schizophrenia (which at that time referred to all psychotic illness) stemmed from childhood experiences, specifically from a smothering, anxiety-ridden mother. But the pendulum took a huge swing in the other direction over the next twenty years; nearly all psychoanalytic theories about mental illness are now out the window, replaced with neurochemical explanations. Magnetic resonance imaging, PET scanning, and other technologies have helped bolster the biological argument by revealing neurological abnormalities in schizophrenic brains. Schizophrenia, says the National Alliance for the Mentally Ill, a vigorous, 170,000-member lobbying group, is a "biologically-based brain disease." This is widely considered to be a liberating notion since alternative explanations in effect assign blame for the disease to a parent or to the person afflicted. The neurochemical focus has also led to a new wave of antipsychotic miracle drugs that have pulled in people like Joshua from their unmoored, storm-tossed voyages of madness and given them a chance to start rebuilding their sanity one block at a time. Joshua firmly believes that antipsychotic drugs saved his life.

But there have also been attempts to look at psychosis in other, broader terms. Throughout the past few decades, some psychiatrists and psychologists have dealt with the borderland between psychosis and mysticism. In the 1960s and 1970s psychiatrists R. D. Laing and John Perry became famous for antipsychiatry crusades; both accused their profession of pigeonholing the psychotic as diseased and thus fundamentally different from, and inferior to, so-called normal people. A schizophrenic may indeed be *mad*, Laing has said, but he is not *ill*. The mind as a whole—including the unconscious, the place of dreams and phantasms and the source of awe—is like an ocean, of which the ego remains mostly ignorant. But a psychotic is in touch with it: he is swimming (one might say drowning) in it. He is not out of his mind but, in fact, *in* his mind; we, the sane, are the ones who are out of our minds, or rather out of touch with most of our minds, in that we can't access them. The psychotic is thus on a profound, dangerous, mystical voyage whose purpose is to find new, deeper ways to communicate. The psychotic isn't content with the ordinary ways of knowing that the ego offers, any more than the religious mystic is.[2] By looking at psychosis as a mere illness, these thinkers said, psychiatry misses the whole point of the affliction: that it is ultimately an attempt to find deeper meaning.

Many of these radical ways of looking at psychotic illness have been reactions to the dominant medical model. Where the recent establishment view is that the problem is in the chemicals, and the solution is likewise a chemical one, these critics have charged that drugs are the enemy, that drugs bring dullness and slowness and the end of all that it means to be human; they can be useful but are ultimately a dangerous short-circuiting of a slower, deeper, more natural process. Such thinking has percolated in the profession for years, but it has remained largely peripheral.

The new wave of thinking that has taken root in recent years is different. It does not reduce the whole business of altered states of mind to drugs, and it also doesn't shy away from drugs: we are physical beings, it says, and as such we have physical brains that work via chemical transactions. But, this new thinking goes, we can also see ourselves as spiritual beings, as having a capacity to transcend ordinary me-in-here/you-out-there ways of knowing. This spiritual side of the human being is tied, in unfathomed ways, to the physical side and to the emotional. If that is so, then the work of a psychiatrist or psychologist goes deeper than those professions have traditionally believed. *Psych*, after all, means "spirit" or "soul," and psychiatry is, etymologically, soul-doctoring. The feeling has grown, especially over the course of the 1990s, that mental health professionals perhaps ought to take a slightly wider view of "abnormal" states of mind.

As an example of this new approach, at Oxford University

in the early 1990s, five thousand psychotic and religious experiences were studied and analyzed for features of both psychopathology and spirituality. One of the findings was that the way an experience is treated by others influences how the subject deals with it. According to British pastoral counselor John Foskett, "If they were listened to and accepted, individuals found ways to integrate even the most disturbing ideas and emotions. If they were ignored or pathologised by others then the trauma was aggravated."[3] Foskett added that "a purely psychiatric approach which explains [the experiences] in terms of dysfunction may actually be instrumental in producing pathological syndromes."

Perhaps more to the point than these findings is the fact that such a study even occurred to anyone and was deemed worth doing.

In his post-psychotic search for a deeper understanding of his psychosis, Joshua eventually found his way to a man who not only proved to be the ideal mentor to a twenty-one-year-old just back from the country of the mad, but who personifies this whole new way of dealing with psychosis and has helped to bring it into the mainstream of his profession.

His name is David Lukoff. Joshua went to Lukoff seeking "validation," and got it. You have been through something akin to Native American vision quests, to shamanism, Lukoff told him. Look at Van Gogh's artwork—he catalogued a similar experience. You can look at it as having to do with your relationship to a higher power. You were clearly in the grip of mental illness, but at least some of the experience was spiritually valuable. Your challenge now is to sort through it, to separate the wheat from the chaff, to isolate where you were onto something good and important, and then to figure out how to use those clues to reorient your life. The challenge is to find the deep meaning in your madness, to let that meaning flow through your whole life, to grow from your madness in ways that you couldn't possibly have grown without it. If you manage to do that, you will find that your illness wasn't a meaningless detour but in fact the most important, most fulfilling event in your life.

David Lukoff is a psychologist at the Saybrook Institute in San Francisco and at the San Francisco Veterans Administration Day Treatment Center. He has served on the faculties of Harvard and UCLA. In 1994, he, along with psychiatrists Francis Lu and Robert Turner, achieved a career-capping milestone when the American Psychiatric Association added to the fourth edition of the *Diagnostic and Statistical Manual of Mental Disorders* (DSM), the bible of the field, a new diagnostic category that they had proposed. This category, the "religious or spiritual problem," while largely symbolic since it is not a billable diagnosis, has been like a hole punched through a wall. Suddenly psychiatrists were authorized to deal with issues of religion and spirituality as such, rather than translating them into the language of psychopathology. The establishment of the new category was covered not just in the *Psychiatric News*, but in the *New York Times*, where it was heralded as a sign that the field of psychiatry, traditionally so narrowly focused on the biomedical model, was opening itself up to religious experience.

At fifty, a thin-boned, neat, studious-looking man, David Lukoff is one of the leaders of the new spiritually attuned psychology. He writes and lectures to colleagues on the historic implications of this change; he has worked for years with people in the depths of psychosis; he more than any other single person brought the new DSM category into being. But he had other, more personal reasons for being interested in Joshua Beil's story. Joshua's appearance in his life took him back to the hippie-era roots of the current fascination with psychosis and to his own early adulthood. "When I heard his story," Lukoff said, "it was déjà vu."

Lukoff's own experience with psychosis came in 1971. The Beatles had just split up; Jim Morrison, Janis Joplin, and Jimi Hendrix had all recently died; the sixties were over, though millions of kids weren't ready for that news. In Cambridge, Massachusetts, twenty-three-year-old David Lukoff had just made the momentous decision to drop out of a doctoral program in anthropology at Harvard. He was an intellectual and intensely serious young man and had been on a firm course to follow in his father's footsteps and become a career academician, when suddenly it occurred to him that he was in danger of missing out on the whole flower-power, free-love experience. In one fateful swoop he gave the university his notice, sold everything he owned, and started hitchhiking across the country. He let his hair grow, consciously identified "not with the hippies but with the freaks." He began reading Zen popularizer Alan Watts, listening to the Grateful Dead, the Jefferson Airplane, and Cat Stevens. He met a girl, they took LSD together. She introduced him to a young would-be guru who had a plan to start a "growth center" as part of the encounter group movement. He invited Lukoff to be a part of it, and Lukoff was thrilled at the idea.

A few days later, in an apartment in Palo Alto, Lukoff woke up in the middle of the night flushed with a strange energy. He went to the bathroom, looked in the mirror: "I noticed that my right hand was giving off a white glow. My thumb and forefinger were touching in the ancient mudra position of the meditating Buddha, and I immediately realized that I was the reincarnation of both Buddha and Christ."

From this moment, his life was transformed. He all but stopped sleeping as he devoted himself to writing in a journal—writing that he soon became convinced would be a new New Testament, a book that would lead to the spiritual renewal of the planet. He held long internal conversations with Bob Dylan, Sigmund Freud, the Buddha, and Christ. He assumed a new identity: The Scholar. The Scholar finished his book, self-published it, mailed copies to friends and family, and waited for the first wave of praise that would steadily grow into global adulation and the lifting-up of The Scholar to the ranks of the great prophets.

Where Joshua Beil spent eight weeks in the throes of his psychosis, Lukoff's episode stretched out over more than six months, and for at least the first two months he maintained a mostly positive feeling that he was growing spiritually enlightened. The growth center became the focus of his thoughts; it was to be established in Chicago, and in his mind Chicago would become "the new Bethlehem," the place from which a new force for spiritual cleansing and reorientation would issue. He slept on friends' sofas, hocked his camera equipment to buy food. His friends didn't think he was crazy—who *wasn't* trying to found a utopian community in 1971? But he also didn't tell anyone that David Lukoff a.k.a. The Scholar was in reality the Buddha/Christ made flesh again. He sensed that others weren't ready to hear that.

Slowly, the experience changed. As months went by and no one called him eager to join the new community he promised to bring about in his book, he picked it up again and reread it. Suddenly it seemed not a vision of world-shaking uniqueness but a painfully naive rehashing of commune-speak and pop utopian ideas. A wave of embarrassment and confusion washed over him. Could it be that The Scholar was not what he had thought? But if The Scholar had been in error, what did that say about his divine underlying self? What exactly had he been doing?

As thoughts of suicide tortured him, he was visited by debilitating headaches and a rare illness called Crohn's disease, which affects the small intestines and causes bleeding and cramps. In the midst of this series of mental and physical ailments, Lukoff says he had the one actual hallucinatory experience of his life. He had flown east and was staying at his parents' summer cottage on Cape Cod trying to get himself together. He was walking along the beach one day when he heard a disembodied voice say to him, "Become a healer." He insists that the voice was human and came from outside him, so that he actually turned around. The effect, he says, was instantaneous; it snapped him out of his recriminations and gave him something to ponder, which he did for many months, since he had never had any thoughts of entering a healing profession.

Jump forward nine years. David Lukoff has become a psychologist and is on the faculty of UCLA. His psychotic episode, which he came to be ashamed of, is well buried, and what he finds remarkable to this day is that "nothing in all my psychological training encouraged me to explore that experience, to see what might be in it." Not only was he not encouraged to explore it, but since at the time any kind of psychotic behavior was labeled schizophrenia, the very idea that that might have been what happened to him "just totally shut me down." Lukoff pointed this out as an example of how much more open psychology and society at large have become in dealing with mental illness as a part of life. "At that time there was a whole literature about 'the abyss of difference' between normal people and psychotics. They were seen as truly different. So if you were a psychology student and you felt you might be suffering from a mental illness, you just shut up about it, you stayed in the closet. Today, I have a student who is completely frank about being a multiple [suffering from multiple personality disorder]. He just sold a book about his life for $500,000, and Robin Williams is supposed to play him in the film."

But Lukoff did begin to deal with what had happened to him, in an indirect way. He had studied behavioral psychology and at UCLA worked under Robert Liberman, a renowned schizophrenia expert. In 1980, Liberman and the Department of Psychiatry won a grant to conduct a study on how social skills training affected people with chronic schizophrenia. The idea was that subjecting the patients to "role-playing exercises" dealing with basic life tasks—returning merchandise, applying for a job—would ease their psychotic symptoms. "The problem was, the study needed a comparison group," Lukoff said. "But what would the comparison group do to fill the hours?"

Lukoff began coming up with ideas: they could put the schizophrenic comparison group on an exercise regimen, teach them meditation. He had been reading literature on holistic approaches to cancer, which, among other things, suggested that it was helpful for patients to find meaning in their illness. Lukoff suggested applying this to schizophrenia; following R. D. Laing and John Perry, whose books on treating psychosis therapeutically and nonjudgmentally rather than chemically were de rigueur reading in the fringes of the profession in the 1970s, he suggested that the control group be encouraged to explore their psychotic symptoms. The study was conducted with Lukoff heading the comparison group, and the result was something that was not supposed to happen: the comparison group actually showed slightly more improvement than the social skills group. This was despite the fact that institutional features of the hospital worked against Lukoff's treatment plan: for example, as he wrote in a paper on the results in *Schizophrenia Bulletin*, "The staff's policy of ignoring all discussion of hallucinations and delusions may have undermined the holistic treatment goal of facilitating acceptance and positive attitudes toward psychotic experiences."[4]

The study was enlightening for Lukoff, both professionally

and personally. He started to think more about what had happened to him nine years earlier and to entertain the possibility that it was indeed a psychotic experience, that there might have been something valuable in it but that his profession simply didn't acknowledge this kind of interpretation. He read about, and was inspired by, the poet Allen Ginsberg's psychotic episode, in which Ginsberg heard the voice of William Blake, and which Ginsberg chose to treat not as a sign of mental illness but as an aesthetic catalyst, as his poetic muse. Ginsberg preserved the event in verse:

Now I'll record my secret vision, impossible sight of the face
    of God:
It was no dream, I lay broad waking on a fabulous couch in
    Harlem
having masturbated for no love, and read half naked an open
    book of Blake on my lap
Lo & behold! I was thoughtless and turned a page and gazed
    on the living Sun-flower
and heard a voice, it was Blake's, reciting in earthern measure:
the voice rose out of the page to my secret ear never heard
    before—
I lifted my eyes to the window, red walls of buildings flashed
    outside, endless
    sky sad in Eternity
sunlight gazing on the world, apartments of Harlem standing
    in the universe—
each brick and cornice stained with intelligence like a vast
    living face—
the great brain unfolding and brooding in wilderness!—now
    speaking aloud with Blake's voice—
Love! thou patient presence & bone of the body! Father! thy
    careful watching and waiting over my soul!

My son! My son! the endless ages have remembered me! My
    son! My son! Time howled in anguish in my ear!
My son! My son! my father wept and held me in his dead
    arms.[5]

Like Ginsberg, Lukoff had felt a wondrous knowledge of the interconnectedness of all things while he was in the state. Like Ginsberg, he had heard a voice, which had called him to his profession. Lukoff came in contact with clinicians who allied themselves with a new school of psychology, which derived from the work of the humanistic psychologist Abraham Maslow.

In the 1950s Maslow revived a line of inquiry begun by William James at the turn of the century, when he attempted to subject religious experience to clinical examination. After studying hundreds of self-described spiritually alive or "self-actualized" people, Maslow wrote his book *Religions, Values, and Peak-Experiences*, in which he claimed that all of these people had had "peak experiences"—a term that encompasses religious epiphany and deep insight. Peak experiences, Maslow argued, are part of the biological, genetic makeup of all human beings; they can be examined and explained empirically as well as religiously. One could reduce all religions to them, if one were of a reductionist mind. But Maslow thought it better to give both religion and science their respective dignity, to consider "peak experience" an empirical way to understand a phenomenon that may be envisioned differently in religious terms.

Maslow defined a peak experience as a personal state of awareness with several characteristics. In a peak state, one has a wider awareness of being; one sees things not in terms of how they affect us but on something like their own terms. The peak experience is also "felt as a self-validating, self-justifying moment." It is felt to be a reason to live. It is an end in itself. "To say this in a negative way, I would guess that peak-experiences help to prevent suicide." Maslow went so far as to say that "peak experiences are one part of the operational definition of the statement that 'life is worthwhile' or 'life is meaningful.' " Time is distorted in a peak experience, and may appear not to exist. "Phrased positively, this is like experiencing universality and eternity."

There are certain values that the peak experience opens one to. They include Truth, Goodness, Beauty, Aliveness, Perfection, Justice, Order, Simplicity, Richness. These are words that subjects gave Maslow when he asked them how the world looked from a peak experience. They correspond, he wrote, to "what people through the ages have called eternal verities, or spiritual values." Related to all of this is the idea of heaven. "The conception of heaven that emerges from the peak experiences is one which exists all the time all around us. . . ."[6]

Maslow's book appeared in 1964, and it became the foundational text for a new movement in psychology. Throughout the 1960s, Maslow and several kindred spirits in psychology—including Stanislav Grof, who would later become renowned for the work he was then carrying out with LSD and breathing techniques as ways to transcend ordinary states of consciousness, and Viktor Frankl, the existentialist Holocaust survivor and author of the classic *Man's Search for Meaning*—held a series of informal meetings in California to find a way to move psychology out of the narrow straits in which they felt it was mired. All agreed that there was a level of human experience that traditional psychology ignored, and that what characterized it was a sense of transcending the individual or personal. Psychology already recognized the so-called pre-personal state of infancy, the period in which the infant has not become conscious of itself as a distinct individual. Then came the personal state of consciousness, in which we live most of our lives and in which we see ourselves as defined by the boundaries of our skin and the privacy of our thoughts. The California group proposed a new movement—transpersonal psychology—that would deal with states of consciousness beyond the personal. An Association for Transpersonal Psychology came into being, and a periodical, the *Journal of Transpersonal Psychology*.

Throughout the 1970s and 1980s, transpersonal psychology provided a kind of organizational backbone to the New Age movement. It was largely ignored by the psychological and psychiatric establishments, and if its practitioners wanted to gain broad acceptance for its underlying message they perhaps might have exercised a little reserve and not embraced everything from spirit channeling to interspecies communication with whales and dolphins. But it survived. Today the body of transpersonal literature continues to grow steadily, and transpersonal authors are in demand as speakers. Lukoff says he keeps "one foot in transpersonal and one foot in mainstream psychology."

In the mid-1980s, Lukoff began working more intensively with psychotic patients and encouraged them to talk about their hallucinations, which got him into trouble with his supervisors at UCLA. "The code was, if a patient started to get delusional, you were supposed to say, in a loud voice, 'It's snowing in Bakersfield.' Of course, it never snows in Bakersfield: it was a signal to the staff that the patient was to be put on extinction. This was standard behavioral theory, that you were supposed to extinguish the delusions by talking about the weather and so on. And here I was telling these people that Allen Ginsberg had had the same thing and became a great poet. 'You can do art and grow from your experience.' "

He designed and taught a course on psychotic hallucinations, in which he had chronically ill people present their "worlds" to psychology graduate students. He did clinical research on psychotic and mystical states and concluded that there is a large area of overlap between the two but that they are not identical. In his practice, he roamed across the traditional boundary between doctor and patient and stressed the need to "join"—to get himself tangled up in a patient's delusional system. One thing that brought him to this risky tack was the idea that the best guide to lead a person back from uncharted territory was someone who had been there himself. But he also had a genuine scientific thirst to explore the unknown. "When I'm working with someone who is delusional, I will actually flip over and try to experience things their way. I think most therapists don't feel comfortable with that, but I take their experience very seriously as a view of reality."

Over time, Lukoff became known for both his radical risk-taking approach to dealing with psychotics and for his refusal to abandon the mainline dictates of psychiatry and psychology. He values the neurochemical way of understanding the problem and thinks his colleagues only do harm when they overvalue it, when they treat it as the only way of understanding mental illness. As he gained renown, curious letters began showing up in his mailbox; his answering machine filled with desperate messages from people who were hungry for a redefining of traditional categories.

Susan Anderson, an artist in Portland, Oregon, looked him up when she was dissatisfied with the way her psychiatrist dealt with a psychotic episode she had had in 1989. Like Joshua Beil, she sought out Lukoff for validation and has since "evolved into a new person," who feels in touch with God in a way she never did before her illness. She has written a book about what she calls her "spiritual crisis."

Paul Levy also contacted Lukoff. In 1981, shortly after graduating from college and while he was teaching painting and drawing at the University of California at Berkeley, Levy was "hit by a lightning bolt. Not literally, but it was like that:

just a split-second experience." Over the next few days he became progressively more "joyful and unrepressed," until finally a friend brought him into Highland Hospital in Oakland. While in the doctor's office, he watched a current of electricity come out of one of his eyes, wrap around the frame of a Van Gogh print on the wall, and come into the other eye. He has had repeated episodes since then and has been hospitalized at least six times with what psychiatrists consistently label as bipolar disorder (the newer term for manic depression). But through all of these episodes Levy says he heard voices, which he took to be the voices of spiritual leaders, telling him that he was "waking up." His spiritual awakening took place over the course of more than ten years, and by the end of it he realized that he could be helpful to people who were going through something similar. "The fact is," he said, "you get no help from a psychiatrist, unless you luck out and get someone like Dr. Lukoff. There are so many people out there having spiritual emergences and not knowing it. They follow their doctor's advice and suppress the process, and that eventually leads to more harm."

Levy developed a full-time noncredentialed practice in Portland, Oregon, leading classes in spiritual awakening and counseling individuals. He sees his episodes most especially in terms of Buddhist ideas of awakening; he has been a practitioner of Tibetan Buddhism since shortly after the first episode, and is the head of the Portland Buddhist Center. "I was told by psychiatrists that I had this incredible, lifelong illness," he said, "and I managed to grow right through it and access the creative energies."

• • •

The various strands of David Lukoff's work—his teaching, his clinical research, his freelance counseling of over-the-transom callers—came together when the DSM task force approved the new diagnostic category in 1994. The approval, which came just months after the meeting between the APA president and the pope, gave Lukoff and the psyche-spirit movement an establishment seal of approval; it made concrete what had been an amorphous longing on the part of mostly isolated individuals in the field. Francis Lu, a psychiatrist at San Francisco General Hospital and clinical professor of psychiatry at the University of California, San Francisco, was, along with Robert Turner, also a psychiatrist at U.C. San Francisco, Lukoff's partner in getting the DSM category established. "Before this category, there was no way to acknowledge a religious or spiritual problem," Lu said. "There was no way for a psychiatrist to deal with loss or questioning of faith, for example, or someone's questioning the beliefs and practices of their church. So the field tended to leave people with the idea that whenever a religious or spiritual issue came up it was either psychopathological, because psychiatry has historically pathologized spirituality, or it was left to the side."

For Lu, the new category allows for some intriguing mixtures of psychiatry and religious exploration. "You can diagnose a mental disorder, like major depression, and concurrently you can diagnose religious or spiritual problems. So the psychiatrist could prescribe antidepressants and engage in psychotherapy, and at the same time make an appropriate referral to, perhaps, a minister or spiritual advisor, who could attend to these issues." Lu acknowledges that the new category is only a first step, but, he says, "it is a very significant one, and many people recognize it as one."

Eugene Kelly, a professor of counseling at George Washington University and the author of *Spirituality and Religion in Counseling and Psychotherapy*, puts it in historic terms. "If you were to look at Freud's work, he was rooted in the intellectual world of his time, which was one of philosophical atheism. And psychology developed as an empirical science, with the focus on behavior. In the early days of the profession there was a lot of interest in psychology and religion, but then it fell off, and behaviorism and Freud kept it on the back burner. But now it's coming back, and that little diagnostic category in the DSM-IV is the tip of the iceberg, I believe."

The category is not one of those that a doctor can use for billing insurance companies so it will probably have little practical utility. Its real value—like that of the meeting between the psychiatrist and the pope—is in signaling a change of perception. It gives credibility to the idea that the human being is made up not only of biological, emotional, and social forces but includes something that transcends the personal and has to do with an individual's intuition of being part of the universe, of being connected to all of life. So psychology has reached a milestone. What were once fringe longings have now found their way into the very heart of the modern science of the individual.

Then again, this milestone looks familiar: we've passed this way before. If David Lukoff and his like-minded colleagues have ushered in a new era, they have also reconnected their profession with its roots. They have taken us back to the early days of psychology, to the time before Freud, and the metaphysical explorations of a century ago.

2

The Singular Pluralism of William James

All for one, one for all.

—ALEXANDRE DUMAS

They were heady, turbulent times. The United States government got involved in a war to preserve American interests, forced itself on a small nation in Southeast Asia, and instigated a popular outpouring against American imperialism. Women were demanding equal rights. Liberal newspapers ran articles decrying the mistreatment of blacks in parts of the South. A president was assassinated.

The decade was not the 1960s but the 1900s. Free love, free will, tearing down the old order: the twentieth century's first flowering of radicalism came with the generation that predated World War I. If you were young and tuned in in, say, 1907, you welcomed the collapse of Victorian values, raised your fist for women's suffrage, fumed at American military presence in the Philippines, attended politically and sexually daring plays by Shaw, Ibsen, and Wilde, were entranced by the rule-breaking art of the post-Impressionists and confused by something new called Cubism.

The American thinker whose ideas inspired you, and who seemed most fully to capture the boldness and expansiveness of the age, was William James. He was an anomaly, a Harvard professor of philosophy who was also a lecturer to audiences of teachers, businessmen, and housewives. His subjects were varied: the evils of American military expansionism, the practical uses of psychology, theories of education, the validity of religious experience. His books were so popular that he once joked, "I begin to look down on Mark Twain!"[1]

James was arguably *the* American intellectual of the time. He actually coined the term, lifting it from the French, where it was used as a derogative, polishing it and putting it to idealistic purposes. In James's view, this new being, the intellectual, worked and sweated as hard as any laborer to produce *ideas*, then whittled and honed them and put them in the service of humanity. The intellectual's enemy was "the institution," be it church, government, or business. "Only in the free personal relation is full ideality to be found," James wrote. Translation: Down with the Establishment!

That kind of sentiment, backed up by a first-rate mind, was enough to inspire a generation of radicals and freethinkers. John Dewey, Robert Frost, Gertrude Stein, and Walter Lippmann were all students or admirers who carried James's philosophy with them as they hewed new paths in art, academia, politics, and life. When, in 1907, after years of delivering his message in lectures at Harvard, James traveled to New York City to teach a semester at Columbia University, he was met by mobs of citizens and a circle of news photographers and feted by the city's elite. Every lecture was filled to capacity, with crowds of students jamming the hallways and spilling out of the building.

And what was this new philosophy? In a word: pluralism. A *Pluralistic Universe* was the title of the last book James published before he died, and it summed up his view of what reality is and how human beings relate to it, participate in it, and make it. The intellectual universe of the late nineteenth century was both materialistic and monotheistic: a good, intelligent Christian or Jew, whether in Cleveland or Paris, believed in the God of Israel and the materialistic reality of science. If there was tension between the two, one struggled to resolve it. For many intellectuals, science won.

James thought the debate between science and religion was nonsense, and that the nonsense was equally distributed. "Damn the absolute!" he liked to declaim in his lectures. Scientific materialism has no right to claim for itself absolute truth, for as it examines the world in its supposedly objective manner it overlooks the fact that the examination is being performed by a decidedly nonobjective entity—an individual human being. The subjective, James argued, from his first days at Harvard to the end of his life, is an utterly inseparable part of experience. However convenient it might be to do so, science cannot separate the "I" from the "it":

> [I]t is absurd for science to say that the egotistic elements of experience should be suppressed. The axis of reality runs solely through the egotistic places—they are strung upon it like so many beads. To describe the world with all its various feelings of the individual pinch of destiny, all the various spiritual attitudes, left out from the description—they being as describable as anything else—would be something like offering a printed bill of fare as the equivalent for a solid meal.[2]

As James put it in A *Pluralistic Universe*, "Which part of [external reality] properly is in my consciousness, which out? If I name what is out, it already has come in."[3] That may sound overly cute or like a hair-splitting side issue, but James believed it was the whole ball game, and elements of his "radical empiri-cism" foreshadowed much of twentieth-century thought. We have a vicious tendency to believe that each thing we see out there in the world is separate and distinct from all else, when common sense shows that that isn't the case. An apple today will be soil next year; things literally are not what they appear to be. The words in our language and the concepts of science are mere conveniences, ad hoc solutions to the problems of living, and should be realized as such. The only thing that we can say is really real, truly true, is *pure experience*. What is real is the flow, the constant but ever-changing pageant comprised of minds and things. "The knower is an actor, and coefficient of the truth on one side, whilst on the other he registers the truth which he helps to create."[4]

This has a ring of both Eastern and Einsteinian philosophy about it. "The Buddhist does not believe in an independent or separately existing external world, into whose dynamic forces he could insert himself," wrote the Tibetan lama Anagarika Govinda. "The external world and his inner world are for him only two sides of the same fabric. . . ."[5] The physicist Werner Heisenberg made nearly the same point: "Natural science does not simply describe and explain nature; it is part of the inter-play between nature and ourselves."[6] James was one of those thinkers who prepared the soil for the philosophy of nondual-ism to take root in the West—the idea that, despite ordinary appearances, our inner life and the outer life of the world are deeply interrelated, that, in some sense, All is One.

But James didn't want to jump from this position to that of, for example, Hindu philosophy, which holds that the external world is an illusion. That kind of idealism was, to him, just as repellent as that of the nineteenth-century scientist, who insisted that the external world was the only reality. We aren't smart enough, James held, to make either of those judgments;

rather, reality seems to take many different forms, and so the best position is for us "to allow the world to have existed from its origin in pluralistic form, as an aggregate or collection of higher and lower things and principles, rather than as absolutely unitary fact."[7]

Put in practical terms, James's pluralism meant that no one dogma—religious, political, racial, aesthetic—could claim to be absolute. As the century progressed, his pluralistic universe divided itself into many smaller pluralisms, each of which has affected who and what we are. The evolving philosophy of religious pluralism, the seed of which later theologians such as Reinhold Niebuhr credited to James, came to guide the course of liberal Protestantism through the century.

Religious pluralism was central to James's philosophy because, as he saw it, religion was central to humanity. If the *universe* was many-sided, then God had to be too. Moreover, the religious impulse, as a phenomenon that occurs in all societies, ought to be in the scientific field of vision. The typical nineteenth-century intellectual may have had scruples against contaminating science with religion, but James did not.

Throughout the 1880s and 1890s, while he was gaining prominence at Harvard with his magisterial *Principles of Psychology*, based in part on dissection of human brains, James was also clipping curious life stories from newspapers and magazines and collecting tales from textbooks, chapbooks, and history books. James was as certain as the other leaders in psychology that the field had to look to biological processes to understand the functioning of personality—*Principles* gives a comprehensive analysis of current thinking on the localization of functions in the brain, including the touch-center and hearing-center, as well as theories about the function of the two hemispheres—but he was just as convinced that science ought to move in other directions at the same time and treat other topics as worthy of investigation. Grace. Saintliness. Soul sickness. Mysticism. *Samadhi*. Nirvana. Agape. What did these terms connote in real life? How did religious conversion actually work? Was it possible to approach religious states of consciousness in nontraditional ways, such as by inhaling nitrous oxide? Was an alcoholic merely a misguided mystic? In venturing into these areas, James made the argument that psyche-spirit researchers today rely on: that to ignore the vast pools of evidence, throughout time and across all human cultures, in which people claim to have had religious experiences of one type or another, is not to do strict science, limiting oneself to just the facts, but indeed to be unscientific, to ignore data that doesn't fit conveniently into one's models.

The challenge, James insisted, was to study both brain physiology and mystical accounts by saints and ordinary people, and to try to create new psychological models that would take both into account. In 1898 he was invited to give the Gifford Lecture on Natural Religion at the University of Edinburgh, in Scotland. The Gifford Lecture was, and is, one of the great honors of academia, offered to someone who has made important contributions to the advance of religious thought. One reason James was chosen to give the lecture lay in his eminently scientific *Principles of Psychology*. After valiantly exploring the known universe of biological knowledge on the subject of how information is processed, the book delves into the philosophical terrain of the mind-body problem, specifically how the mind and brain connect. After showing how difficult it is to demonstrate how or where or even whether the biological organ called the brain hooks up to a nonbiological idea-factory called the mind, James takes the strikingly bold step, for a scientist and philosopher, of introducing "soul" into the picture.

All mind-body theories are so hopelessly confused, he states, that bringing in the concept of soul is "the line of least logical resistance, so far as we yet have attained." Psychologically speaking, says the greatest of American psychologists, following out all major theories of how the mind works leads one to "the logical respectability of the spiritualistic position."[8]

It was this openness to religiosity in the heart of the great textbook of psychology that led the Gifford committee to ask James to give the course of lectures in Scotland. What he gave them drew more on his years of clipping of case histories than on his years of brain research. For two seasons in 1901 and 1902 James held an audience of several hundred professors and students in rapt attention as he laid out his elaborate argument for taking religion seriously as an area of scientific study.

In print those lectures became *The Varieties of Religious Experience*; the book is a loose but sustained argument for taking science broad rather than narrow. James appointed himself the enemy of what he called medical materialism: the view, then as now common among scientists and many of the rest of us, that biological explanations trump all others. "Medical materialism finishes up Saint Paul by calling his vision on the road to Damascus a discharging lesion of the occipital cortex, he being an epileptic," James wrote. "It snuffs out Saint Teresa as an hysteric, Saint Francis of Assisi as an hereditary degenerate."[9] James didn't argue with the idea that these mystics may have suffered from organic ailments, but he refused to accept that a medical condition invalidated a spiritual one.

James's challenge was to be true to science, strictly defined, while at the same time being true to our inner convictions. He would resist the temptation to reduce religious experience to some snowstorm in the brain, which was easy enough to do even then but which he saw was really playing with a stacked deck, since medical materialism decides the outcome of all such cases in advance. Besides that, what insight have you gained, he wondered, by concluding that "William's melancholy about the universe is due to bad digestion"?[10] William may in fact have bad digestion, but there is still the universe to contend with.

So James challenged psychologists to keep the balls of biology, psychology, and spirituality in the air. He studied the case of George Fox, the founder of Quakerism, and tried to account for the fact that all who knew him found him to be a riveting, deeply spiritual person, but that at the same time, as James writes, "from the point of view of his nervous constitution, Fox was a psychopath, or détraqué of the deepest dye."[11] Religion is one part of the definition of healthy humanity, yet many of the great spiritual figures of history seem to have been, by any measurable criteria, out of their minds. James insisted on keeping his focus wide enough to acknowledge both sides of this equation, and so set the challenge that psychologists today have taken up in large numbers, after having ignored it for most of this century.

How recent is that sea change? Martin Marty, the University of Chicago historian of religion, in his 1982 introduction to *Varieties*, was able to call the book "a classic that is too psychological to have shaped most religious inquiry and too religious to have influenced much psychological research." Today that statement seems as outmoded as Victorian headgear. *Varieties* has become James's most read book, and it is probably the single most influential book among spiritually oriented psychologists.

Put another way, it is only now that James's pluralism bullet, which has had such an impact in so many fields, is hitting home in psychology.

•   •   •

The ironic thing about James's pluralistic, radically empirical, spirit-welcoming philosophy was that, for all his attention to individual religious experience, deep down William James was a soul mate, so to speak, of that famous atheist, Sigmund Freud. Freud, after pondering a friend's description of religiosity as an "oceanic feeling," famously remarked, "I cannot discover this 'oceanic' feeling in myself."[12] James confessed his own absence of religious feeling similarly: "My personal position is simple. I have no living sense of commerce with a God ... yet there is *something in me* which *makes response* when I hear utterances from that quarter made by others. I recognize the deeper voice. Something tells me: '*thither lies truth*'—and I am sure it is not old theistic prejudices of infancy." He added, with touching self-deprecation, "Call this, if you like, my mystical *germ*. It is a very common germ."[13]

Freud's lack of belief, however, was utterly different. It was a banner, a crusade. Freud appeared on the scene, with the timing of a Hollywood antagonist, just when it seemed that James's influence might transform psychology, at least in the United States. Freud was twelve years younger than James, and his rise to fame roughly corresponded to James's: his *Principles of Psychology* appeared in 1890; Freud's *Interpretation of Dreams*, which would change the course of psychology and of the twentieth century, was published in 1900. Freud's mind was more in step with the science of the times. James's expansive sensibility—"Every bit of us at every moment is part and parcel of a wider self "[14]—led him to mix and bend traditions at will. Any one of his books contains elements of philosophy, psychology, physiology, religious speculation, and even autobiography. Such an interdisciplinary approach would not be out of place in a consciousness studies graduate program today, but at the turn of the century the trend was toward compartmentalizing. (Soon after James's time psychology would break free of the Department of Philosophy at Harvard and become a separate discipline.)

Freud, however, was very much a man of his time—a time when science and atheism went hand in hand among Europeans of a certain class. People tend to forget that before he became the founder of psychoanalysis Freud was an M.D. He operated a renowned practice from his home-office apartment suite in a residential neighborhood of Vienna and was also attached as a physician to the Kassowitz Institute, a children's hospital. He was a respected member of Austria's Imperial Society of Physicians. He coauthored a book on cerebral palsy in children. In short, he was a member of the medical establishment, and as such was disposed to take a practical view of science. In fact, he thought that brain chemistry was the key to unlocking the mysteries of personality. He believed that one day neurology would end the sufferings of the madmen raving in locked wards, of guilt-ridden adulterers and hypochondriac hausfraus. "The future," he wrote, "may teach us to exercise a direct influence, by means of particular chemical substances." It was out of frustration with the primitive state of neurology that he searched for other solutions to the puzzle of the human being.

In 1882, Freud had met the physician Josef Breuer, and through him became interested in the possibilities of psychotherapy. In 1885 he traveled to Paris, where he became a professional devotee of the renowned French neurologist Jean-Martin Charcot and soon adopted Charcot's fascination with hysteria. Hysteria is now called somatization disorder; it refers to a cluster of extreme physical ailments for which there is no known organic cause: pain, vomiting, sexual dysfunction, dizziness, blindness, seizures. It used to be thought that only women suffered from it, thus the old term, which derives from *hystera*, Greek for uterus. Charcot made a specialty of male hysteria, specifically "hysterical paralysis," such as the sudden loss of use of a limb, and demonstrated that it resulted from psychological trauma, not, as was then thought, from nerve damage. One of Charcot's techniques for creating a temporary hysterical paralysis—and thus showing how the mind could control the body—was hypnosis.

Over the course of the next decade, Freud refined the techniques of hypnosis and psychotherapy and widened his interests to include phobias and other psychological phenomena. While going through his own psychological crisis in the late 1890s, and in the course of conducting the most famous self-analysis in history, Freud began to focus his attention on his own dreams. On July 23, 1895, he had a dream in which a woman named Irma was receiving an injection. He realized that it pertained to an episode in his life: he had recently called on his friend Wilhelm Fliess to perform an operation on one of his patients, and Fliess had botched the job. The Irma dream represented Freud's unconscious attempt to defend Fliess. This became "the dream" in psychoanalytic lore, the one that convinced Freud that dreams were the key to unlock the cabinet of the unconscious.

The Interpretation of Dreams, which claimed that dreams are "wish fulfillment," was published in 1900, and with it, one could argue (Freud did), a new science, the science of psychoanalysis, was born. Of course, movements take time to build— the initial print run of *Interpretation of Dreams,* a scant six hundred copies, had not sold out two years later. By 1907, however, the Wednesday-night discussion group that met at Freud's apartment had evolved into the Vienna Psychoanalytical Society, and a year later an International Congress of Psychoanalysis convened. Freud's brainchild was about to take the scientific world by storm, to change a century's worth of minds on the subject of the mind.

But the wider, Jamesian perspective in psychology, the one that held that our individual selves are all part of "a wider self," did not go down without a fight. At the last moment a challenger stepped forward to take on the man who would be king. By 1909 Freud had already anointed Carl Jung his "successor and crown prince," who would carry the new science of psychoanalysis into the future. Jung too was a medical man—he was a psychiatrist before becoming interested in psychoanalysis—but from an early age he, like James, was intellectually drawn to spiritual matters.

As Freud's friend as well as the founder and first president of the International Psychoanalytic Association, Jung was well positioned to encourage Freud to broaden some of his terminology and so allow the new field to roam into the territory of religion and spirituality. But it seemed neither man had any idea of the depth of the other's feelings on the subject. During a meeting in Freud's office in 1909, the chasm suddenly stretched open.

According to Jung, it was a thump behind a bookshelf that led to one of the most storied breakups in history. He had asked the master what he thought about parapsychology. Besides having an interest in with spiritualism, Jung had studied Chinese literature, especially *The Secret of the Golden Flower* and the *I Ching*, which led to an interest in what he referred to as "meaningful coincidences" (for which he was later to coin the term synchronicity). One example is the ritual practice, outlined in the *I Ching*, of using the fall of sticks and toss of coins as oracles to guide one's decision making.

Jung came to believe that there is a relatedness of events that occur in a given time, a kind of subterranean connection, and this helped convince him that psychology should not limit itself to the individual personality. He wanted to know the master's thoughts on the subject.

Freud embarked on a long answer, the upshot of which was that he believed such things were nonsense. "While Freud was going on in this way," Jung recalled in *Memories, Dreams, Reflections*, "I had a curious sensation. It was as if my diaphragm were made of iron and were becoming red-hot—a glowing vault. And at that moment there was such a loud report in the bookcase, which stood right next to us, that we both started up in alarm, fearing the thing was going to topple over on us. I said to Freud: 'There, that is an example of a so-called catalytic exteriorization phenomenon.'"

"Oh come," Freud replied, and added (in Richard and Clara Winston's translation), "That is sheer bosh."[15]

But Jung believed in what he had said, and he predicted it would happen again, which, according to his memory, it did. (Freud later sent Jung a note to say that the knocks had continued long after Jung left, which apparently did not change Jung's mind.)

The split between Freud and Jung occurred on many levels and took place over a period of years, but it can be traced back to a basic difference of opinion on how to define the human being. At one level, the disagreement was about the importance of sexuality: Jung didn't give it the primacy that Freud did. But, put another way, the libido debate was really about spirituality: Jung expanded Freud's definition of libido beyond the boundaries that Freud was comfortable with, until it came to mean something like life force: "Libido is the energy which is able to communicate itself to any field of activity whatsoever, be it power, hunger, hatred, sexuality or religion."[16]

After the knock-on-the-wall incident, Freud and Jung were never again on the same easy terms, and by 1913 the split was final. "[T]his incident aroused his mistrust of me," Jung wrote, "and I had the feeling that I had done something against him."[17]

Psychology and its related professions, along with much of the Western world, followed Freud. That way lay science, reason, the hope of reducing mankind's most private pains to the level of chemistry, and so curing them. William James became enshrined in the history of philosophy for his contributions to American pragmatism, and in psychology for writing the first comprehensive textbook—not, in other words, for his work in psychology and religion. Jung and his followers went subterranean: always there, respected for certain contributions, but seen by many practitioners as something of an embarrassment.

Freud chalked up the episode with the bookshelf as superstition, a reflection on his protégé's mental state. For Jung, however, the incident pointed to profoundly different views not just of human psychology but of reality itself. It was Freud's insistence on the duality of mind and body—on the common-sense distinctness of the inner world of thoughts and the outer world of events—that Jung objected to. Like James, Jung believed that the mind and body—and the individual and the world—are connected in ways science does not imagine, but which the mystical traditions of all religions insist on. Freud, in Jung's view, was limiting the field of psychological inquiry as he sought to define it and make it acceptable to the broader public. Jung insisted that this would cripple both the field and society. If their search was for truth, Jung argued, it would not do to erect for the sake of convenience arbitrary walls, for the truth might well lie beyond them.

But Freud had good reasons for keeping the focus of his new science narrow. Science was Freud's religion; he referred to Darwin and other scientists as "modern saints."[18] He was determined that his intellectual offspring be accepted not as theory or art but as science—and not just any offshoot but a vital part of science, for "its contribution to science consists precisely in the extension of research into the mental sphere."[19] Galileo and Copernicus had taken on the cosmos, Darwin the species; Freud was extending the reach of science into the mind itself.

In an age in which the shelves of any Barnes & Noble are crammed with volumes on Eastern thought, the Cosmic Christ, Native American wisdom, the revival of Jewish mysticism, and how to recognize a Kundalini experience, *The Future of an Illusion*, Freud's antireligion manifesto, published in 1927, comes across as a historical curiosity. Religious beliefs are "illusions," "delusions," "wish fulfillments." They are psychological pacifiers, projections of what we would like to have exist. For civilization to survive, it must renounce these illusions and instead worship "our God, Logos." But the "masses" are "lazy and unintelligent" so it is up to the intellectuals to "set an example" and lead the way.[20]

There was a practical dimension to Freud's determination to keep his definition of the human psyche narrow. For psychoanalysis to be adopted as a science it had to be seen as tied to the prevailing biomedical model; the wall between "me in here" and "that out there" had to stay firmly in place. Freud had big things in mind, bigger than Jung and his other colleagues imagined. He was appealing to the world's academies of science and medicine to accept a new charter member. It was going to be hard enough to get medical men to buy into the notion that their infant sons and daughters had full, rich sex lives. To expect bone-setters and skin plasterers, liver men and blood men, the hard, practical, furrow-browed, and moustachioed men of medicine to go along with a new field that even hinted at the possibility of finding hidden meaning in knocks on a wall—it's a wonder Freud didn't throw his heir apparent bodily out in front of the butcher shop that occupied the ground floor of his Berggasse Street apartment building.

Of course, there was controversy and scandal involved in the birth pangs of psychoanalysis, there were the celebrated attacks (Nabokov called Freud a "witch doctor" and "the Viennese quack") and the newspaper screeds. But as they died down, psychoanalysis grew and became accepted, became a part of life, an essential ingredient in the twentieth-century way of understanding the world. It succeeded so well, in fact, that it fairly swallowed up the already established fields of psychology and psychiatry, and Freud became the undisputed king of the mind. Other major figures in the field—Alfred Adler, Jung, Erik Erikson—whether friend or foe, came to be viewed largely in relation to him: in terms of where their views departed from his, how they modified him.

The anti-Freud era probably began in the late 1970s, as advances in drug therapy shifted the focus in psychiatry to biology. The titles of recent books about Freud and psychoanalysis—*A Most Dangerous Method, Seductive Mirage*—give a clear view of the change of opinion. In 1998 the literary critic Frederick Crews published a devastating compilation of essays attacking every aspect of Freud's work. Crews charged that "our great detective of the unconscious was incompetent from the outset—no more astute, really, than Peter Sellers' bumbling Inspector Clouseau—and that he made matters steadily worse as he tried to repair one theoretical absurdity with another."[21]

On the other hand, psychotherapy and counseling are probably more popular now than ever. According to data from the American Psychological Association, there are more than 300,000 licensed psychiatrists, psychotherapists, and counselors in the United States; by one estimate between ten million and fifteen million Americans are in some kind of formal therapy at any given time, and there are at least two hundred different talking cures being practiced, most of which can trace their theoretical base back to Freud.

That said, psychoanalysis itself has certainly diminished in our day. There are three reasons: the pace of modern life, the rise of psychopharmacology, and the rise of health maintenance organizations. No one has time for full-scale analysis anymore, and even if they did their insurance probably wouldn't cover it. And drug therapy has caught everyone's attention anyway, both in the profession and among the public, as a hard-to-beat shortcut. But in a way, the rise of Prozac and Zoloft and Risperdal and Clozaril is in keeping with Freudian thought. Antipsychotics and antidepressants work thanks to psychiatrists' evolving understanding of how the levels of different neurotransmitters in the synapses between nerve endings affect a person's state of mind. If reuptake sites are blocked chemically, the body's supply of a naturally produced chemical such as serotonin or dopamine builds, which can lift depression and generate feelings of well-being; eliminating surpluses of dopamine can do away with psychotic delusions.[22] In other words, we are now in the early stages of the time that Freud looked forward to, when important elements of personality and disorder can be described and altered in purely biomedical terms.

But, William James might say, just because we *can* describe them solely in such terms does not mean that we should; to think that the rise of the chemical understanding of mental life discounts literal soul-searching is to fall into the trap of medical materialism.

James and Freud met once, at a ceremony at Clark University in Worcester, Massachusetts, in September 1909. Neither man recorded the substance of their conversation, but the meeting itself was one of those, like that of the pope and the psychiatric leader, that symbolize the changing of an age. Just a few months before, Freud had had the knock-on-the-wall meeting with Jung, which had begun the paring-down of supporters of psychoanalysis to only those who remained loyal to Freud's narrow model. James, we know, did not think much of Freud's "fixed ideas," but he was evidently excited and nervous at meeting the famous man. He must have had some sense that the other represented a tidal wave that was about to wash over him.

After the ceremony the two walked more than a mile together to the train station. During the walk James suffered a physical attack that affected his heart and breathing, but he did his best to hide it, as though anxious that the other would read psychological meaning in it—would relate physical frailty to the frailty of Jamesian psychology. Freud graciously pretended to ignore the attack and picked up his colleague's suitcase and carried it the rest of the way. James died less than a year later. Freud lived on.

3

Zeitgeist

> Would it be preposterous to you that, before we
> diagnose seasonal affective disorder, we have to
> rule out first starvation of the spirit, and that
> before we prescribe serotonin reuptake inhibitors
> or megalight, we first prescribe courses on Emer-
> son and Thoreau and lessons in cross-country
> skiing . . . ?
>
> —PAUL FLEISCHMAN, M.D.,
> OSKAR PFISTER AWARD LECTURE DELIVERED TO THE
> AMERICAN PSYCHIATRIC ASSOCIATION, MAY 1993

Unbeknownst to most people, Freud had a kind of Jamesian muse (or thorn) right at his side for most of his professional life. His name was Oskar Pfister, and he was arguably the best friend Freud ever had. He was also the oddest member of Freud's circle: on his first visit to the Berggasse flat, he came across as so exotic that Freud's fourteen-year-old daughter Anna thought him "like an appari-tion from an alien world."[1] Artists, poets, and anarchists were routine visitors to the Freud household, but in that rigorously secular apartment a Protestant pastor, a man of God, seemed downright outlandish.

He was born in Switzerland in 1873 and followed his father in becoming a pastor in Zurich, but at first struggled with the work and with the narrowness of Swiss Protestant theology. He came to study psychology as a way to help him extend his

Christian beliefs into the ordinary lives of his parishioners, but it wasn't until he read Freud that he saw the force of the connection between the psychological man and the spiritual man, the link between the ancient and modern connotations of "psyche," the exploration of which would become his own life's work. In Freud's new science of psychoanalysis, Pfister later wrote, "the highest functions of life stepped before the soul-microscope and gave evidence about their origins and their connections, about the laws of their development, their deeper meaning in the totality of psychic events."[2]

Pfister went on to study and practice psychoanalysis, to write the first textbook on the subject (which was published in 1913), and to befriend Freud. Freud is famous for his intense friendships (with Jung, with Alfred Adler, with Wilhelm Fliess, with Otto Rank) that eventually burst into flames and crashed. Pfister was the only one of his associates with whom he remained close until his death. Their friendship, however, was often a sparring match, for as convinced as Freud was that psychoanalysis was a tool for eradicating religion and other superstition, Pfister was equally convinced that the master had discovered a key to spiritual growth. Freud dismissed his friend's arguments, and the psychotherapeutic professions largely did too for most of the century. But in today's spirit-centered retooling of psychology and psychiatry it is the ghost of Oskar Pfister that hovers more noticeably than that of any of the other, more renowned early practitioners who encircled Freud, because Pfister approached not just the subject but life itself with both intellect and an inner awareness of the divine. In fashioning himself into something Freud might have sworn could not exist—a spiritual psychoanalyst—Pfister perpetuated the Jamesian spirit in psychology.

Evidently, Freud could not entirely tolerate the contradiction that Pfister embodied. He wrote his antireligion manifesto, *The Future of an Illusion,* in part for Pfister, perhaps as what he hoped would be the decisive volley in their ongoing debate. As the book was nearing publication, however, Freud suddenly worried that his friend would be bowled over by it, so he sent him a note warning him that the book "will be painful for you."

But the pastor's capacity to turn the other cheek was astonishing. He read the book cheerfully, countered with a little essay entitled "The Illusion of a Future," and continued to abash Freud by saying of him "a better Christian never was."[3]

Why did Pfister believe psychoanalysis complemented the Bible? Freud said it himself, in a letter to Jung: Psychoanalysis is "essentially a cure through love."[4] For Freud, of course, love was properly understood as the discharge of libido. But this was mere jargon to Pfister, the enforced myopia of a scientist. Psychoanalysis was only a tool; life was bigger than it, and love was the language of life. Freud might want to hem it in with his theories and principles, but love would spill out the sides. It was because Freud had discovered one of the secret subterranean passageways of love that Pfister felt able to call his Jewish atheistic friend a Christian. He meant it as a compliment, of course, but surely he was aware how much it would irk the old man. He was capable of sparring, too.

Freud himself never disappointed Pfister, but by the time Pfister died in 1956 at the age of eighty-three he must have been disappointed that his dream of extending the insights of psychoanalysis into spiritual life had all but vanished.

• • •

As it turns out, Oskar Pfister has not faded entirely into history. In 1983 the American Psychiatric Association began presenting an annual Oskar Pfister Award to an individual who has made "important contributions to the humanistic and spiritual side of psychiatric issues." Interestingly, few Americans and few psychiatrists have received the award. Winners have included the neurologist Oliver Sacks, the German theologian Hans Kung, the developmental faith theorist James Fowler, and psychoanalyst and Holocaust survivor Viktor Frankl.

The man who won the 1993 Pfister Award, Paul Fleischman, happens to be both an American and a psychiatrist, and is in many ways a latter-day Oskar Pfister. Fleischman got his M.D. from the Yale School of Medicine, and upon completing his residency had numerous prestigious job offers in academia. But this was in 1974, and he had spent the height of the hippie era hunkered down in medical studies; like David Lukoff, he was a long-haired type who hadn't had time to go countercultural. Now that he had his M.D., he shocked friends and family by declining all job offers and going to India in search of a spiritual master. He found one, and began what would become a career-long meditation practice that would color his whole approach to psychotherapy, just as Christianity had for Pfister. When he returned to the States, he began teaching a seminar on psychiatry and religion at Yale, and set up a private psychiatry practice.

Fleischman is a small, shy man. In a Chinese restaurant on the Upper West Side of Manhattan, at a lunch in his honor hosted by colleagues, he seemed to duck the gazes of his fellow practitioners. He sat quietly at the center of the long table (something about his size and shyness making him seem older than his fifty-two years), emanating a wiry mass of gray hair and beard, ten delicate fingers wrapped around a porcelain teacup. When he answered questions at lunch and when he spoke at a lecture later that day, his voice was so soft it threatened to merge with the white noise of the background. His eyes, though, blazed.

One might have expected the talk to be something like a traditional lecture. Instead, this onetime member of the clinical faculty of the Yale University School of Medicine gave something closer to a collection of aphorisms. He sat like a guru or a gnome, his body a seeming appendage, and said things like this:

"We need to be upbraided by the incongruous boldness of wrens."

"The deep cultivation of inner peace cannot occur through psychotherapy."

Children should not be shunted from school to playdate to music lesson, but should be allowed to savor the "structureless domes of uninterrupted afternoons."

Clearly, this was a psychiatrist who had transcended the ordinary bounds of his profession. The fullest form of Fleischman's psychospiritual argument is in his 1989 book *The Healing Spirit*, which won him the Pfister Award. Its subtitle is *Explorations in Religion and Psychotherapy*, and the book details, in straightforward manner, how in our everyday lives psychological forces are shot through with religion, and religious issues have psychological dimensions. Fleischman's goal is to explore both ways of knowing without trying to collapse one into the other. As much as he thinks the founders of psychoanalysis erred in ignoring the spiritual, he is also critical of some of his fellow psyche-spirit explorers of today, who would lump the psychological and the spiritual together and try to tell us that they are simply different vocabularies for the same experience. Based on his extensive private practice and his historical study of psychotherapy and religion, and on William James's definition of religion as "man's total reaction upon life," Fleischman isolates what one might call eternal truths: points where psychological truth and spiritual truth overlap. He then shows how the needs that underlie these truths might drive us to either therapy or religion, and how each can help fulfill the need but also how both can twist and distort it. "Lawful order" is one of the ten timeless human needs he describes: we need to feel that things have a sensible structure. A church gives us this spiritually, of course, and physically it is a place, a routine. One of the reasons we go to a therapist is to help us pull the seemingly random events of life into lawful order: to find out the story of our life. A sense of lawful order is necessary to a healthy human life; its absence is almost the textbook definition of insanity.

But both religion and psychotherapy can warp this need, and Fleischman is breathtaking in his elegant critique of how both of these systems can betray us. Anthropomorphic imagery—giving God a face, a character; simply using the word "God" is already a step in this direction—fulfills this need for lawful order, and does so in both psychological and religious ways. Psychologically, "it facilitates a retreat into permanent childhood, in which the unknown is given the mask of a face"—in other words, it allows us to express our smallness and dependence—"and, as the most powerful tool of religious imagination, it lifts our glance upward toward the face of the unknown." But on the other hand, "the need for lawful order may deteriorate into fanciful illusions that an aged adult male is personally witnessing, extending significance to, and running a classroom-world."[5]

Psychologically, the lawful order impulse can ossify into sadism, into the expression of cruel and godlike power over others. Throughout his book, Fleischman moves exquisitely back and forth, letting these two realms inform each other, observing where they penetrate each other but also insisting that they are different.

Perhaps his most moving analysis, and the one that reveals him as a modern Oskar Pfister, is of love. "Every case of psychotherapy, to a greater or lesser extent, is a problem of the failure to love," he writes. One of the most intriguing sentences in the book is this: "My interest in religious issues in psychotherapy has been spurred on by a series of patients who have told me spontaneously, without prompting but after considered thought, that their impaired search for love was floundering because they were seeking religion through sexual intimacy."[6]

That sentence brought to mind a passage from the commentary to an edition of Patanjali's yoga sutras. Patanjali was the Socrates of Hindu tradition, known to history by the sometimes cryptic aphorisms that followers wrote down. In 1953, the novelist and playwright Christopher Isherwood and Hindu scholar Swami Prabhavananda published an annotated edition of the sutras that contained this piece of commentary:

> Some people who have read (and misunderstood) Freud are apt to say sneeringly: "Religion is nothing but repressed sex." And this remark is supposed to shock us into giving up religion in disgust. But it would not have shocked Patanjali in the least, though he might have laughed at its stupidity. "Sex," he would have retorted, "is nothing but potential religion."[7]

The idea behind both of these passages is that the sexual urge and the spiritual urge both partly come from a need not to be alone, a need to connect. Psychotherapy tries to satisfy this need, too. "People may seek religion in sexual activity," Fleischman writes, "and, when that fails, they may seek religion in the cure for failed sexuality, psychotherapy: a serialized error."[8] In a secular society, we may feel the urge not to be alone and incorrectly read it as sexual; and when sex doesn't fulfill us we turn to therapy. Our ingrained individualism has contributed to our confusion: "Contemporary sociologists have pointed to individualism as an isolating, socially fragmenting force, the goal of which is freedom *from* others, rather than freedom *to* be or do."[9] The confusion results from the fact that we are led to believe that we can make it on our own, but we can't because the individual isn't really that—individual being is wrapped up in the being of other individuals, and in Being itself.

Fleischman believes that psychotherapy can help us out of this trap, but it involves letting go of the one apparently irreducible feature of psychological theory: the idea of oneself as an individual. Release is another of Fleischman's basic human needs central to both psychotherapy and religion. Release of tension, of fear, letting consciousness drop off into sleep—these are the common stuff of psychology. But, Fleischman writes, "Release is not limited to the soothing of internal conflict; it includes the ability to accept reality, the inevitable, and the capacity to extend trust toward the world."[10] In this way, psychological release bleeds into spiritual release, the letting-go of the tense little packet I call me. It is not a simple matter of "just relax," however. Spiritual release—giving oneself into God's hands, if you like—comes about through practice, and all religions have developed techniques for achieving it.

Which leads us to Fleischman's chosen spiritual path, and how he relates it to his work as a psychiatrist. He conducted his search for a spiritual path analytically. There would be no messy getting swept up in a cult. The ideal practice would be nonsectarian (he was interested in spirituality, not the baggage of religion). It had to be freely offered, not tainted by money. And it would have to appeal to logic, not simply demand obedience and blind faith. He found Vipassana meditation in 1974 and has been a practitioner of it ever since. He has accepted as his life's path to practice it twice a day for at least an hour at a time, to devote himself to it full-time for between ten and thirty days a year, and to assist at meditation courses another ten days a year. He virtually emanates the practice: it breathes through him, and informs his psychiatric work. "My meditation gives me a sensibility," he said, "an awareness, based upon knowledge of myself, that I can then extend toward others. It is not an ideology, but an attunement."

Vipassana is the meditation technique taught by the Buddha. It is not, Fleischman stresses, Buddhism, which contains a carapace of rituals and beliefs that do not derive from the Buddha, much as Catholicism is layered with traditions that have no direct relationship to the historical Jesus. Fleischman does not consider himself a Buddhist. He does, however, see himself as a scientist, even in his spiritual pursuit. "I'm a scientist, and I'm trying to observe and understand reality. All scientists use tools—microscopes, telescopes. I use Vipassana."

Vipassana is unusually well suited to a scientific temperament because it involves bare observation. A Vipassana meditator simply sits and observes: no mantra, prayer, chant, or posture. What does the meditator observe? Not the mind, but the body. The Vipassana tradition understands something about the nature of reality that classical science did not. "Nineteenth-century scientists believed it was possible to objectively observe the world. In psychiatry, the early Freudians thought they were observing their patients objectively. In the twentieth century, science has realized that actual objectivity isn't possible, and nobody in psychiatry today thinks they are objective observers."

Vipassana understands a basic paradox: The subject cannot become a true object. "If you try to observe your own mind, you find that you can't. The mind will continue to travel, and you will be washed along with it. But we can observe the body, and a Vipassana meditator soon realizes that the body is composed of a vibrating mass of particles. As you get deeper into Vipassana practice, you learn that the changes in the body are the base of mental contents. As I get hungry, my thoughts change. There are millions of occurrences like that which take place at such minute levels you aren't aware of them unless you really focus. It's hard to give examples because these sensations haven't been named—it's like the story of all the names the Eskimos have for snow. The gross sensations are easy: sleep, hunger, sex. But philosophical thinking is also a body sensation. In yoga, you are aware that as you change your body you change your thoughts. And if there is a change in your thoughts—if you suddenly become frightened, for example—your body changes accordingly. The actual chemical makeup of the body is changed by thoughts."

An ongoing practice of Vipassana leads to greater and greater insight into the nature of one's thoughts and feelings. As a result, one becomes a finely tuned observer and a keen empathizer, qualities that naturally make for a better psychotherapist. Beyond that, however, Fleischman insists that Vipassana leads inescapably to ethical conduct: "I'm not going to observe myself and reach the conclusion that I want to be hungry. I'm going to realize that I want peace. I'm going to realize that loving my wife is better than fighting with my wife. So Vipassana leads to the awareness that it is self-serving to be non-self-serving. This paradox is in the Buddha's teaching. It's also in the Boy Scouts' code."

Again, the overlapping ideas of love and release come up, both of which have to do with extending the self toward that which is beyond it: "A spiritual life to me is having a living identification beyond. Beyond me, to my wife. Then beyond our duo to the community. Then beyond the community. You keep going beyond, and wherever it hits a limit, you keep going."

As a psychiatrist, Fleischman tries to help his patients to live this way because, he believes, these are the shared values of psychology and religion. But he does it with the standard tools of psychiatry, not by teaching his patients to meditate or by bringing up overtly spiritual issues. Just as much as he values the spiritual and insists that it gives a grounding of ethics and observation to his work, he also insists on the need for doing psychiatry within professional limits: "A spiritual psychiatrist should first of all be a psychiatrist." He believes in the fifty-minute session, in not seeing patients socially; he prescribes Prozac where he thinks it helpful and resists patients who ask for drugs when he thinks they won't be helpful.

As much as anything else, he insists on getting paid. "The psychotherapist-patient relationship is a paid professional relationship. That is critical. That's what Freud invented. It sets a boundary. I keep going back to payment because the New Age has blurred the boundaries between therapy and spirituality." As an example, he pointed to no-cost psychotherapy, which many people feel is a good and worthy thing but which Fleischman thinks shades dangerously (or at least confusingly) into the territory of religion. He is uncomfortable with the association of the psyche-spirit movement with the New Age movement. The one is a thoughtful, wise, but critical expansion of psychology into the terrain of spirituality; the other, he feels, has too often promoted a flat "anything goes" philosophy. By way of example, he pointed to the current passion for herbal cures, homeopathy, and other new-old remedies: " 'How can I cure my cancer with an herb?' That's not spirituality. Spirituality has to do with the meaning of life. This is something else: a pathetic deviation of the New Age mind-set."

As traditional as he sometimes sounds, though, Fleischman quite cheerfully and radically challenges his profession in some of its most basic assumptions. The goal of trying to make someone who suffers from schizophrenia "normal," which anyone who has sworn allegiance to the Hippocratic oath would probably take as a given, may be misguided. "Autonomy," Fleischman told an audience of his colleagues in accepting the Pfister Award, "is a worthy goal, but not the exclusively valuable human attainment." Some people, he went on, including some schizophrenic patients, "can only be coerced toward autonomy at the expense of their sanity." Psychiatrists should continue to refine their search for antipsychotics and other medicines that can help such people, but they ought also to maintain an "appreciation for lifestyles that are of necessity rooted in passivity, daydreams, varying degrees of dependence, reverie, and speculation."[11]

A mainstream psychiatrist might do a double take here. Is this healer suggesting giving up on his profession's most sacred charter? Might he next counsel that a migraine sufferer learn to enjoy his pain, that someone dying from AIDS come to appreciate the dark beauty of a body wasting away?

No, but in a way he is laying an even greater challenge before his profession, which may be one reason why *Psychiatric Times*, the newspaper of the APA, neglected to cover Fleischman's award and speech. He is saying several things at once here, all of which get underneath the simple layer of curing illness and try to fathom what a doctor's goals are and ought to be in such cases. On one level he is saying that until there is such a thing as a pill that neatly and wholly converts a wayward and delusional mind to health and coherence psychiatrists might do well to let this illness, and the state of consciousness it brings about, teach them something. There are perfectly "normal" people who depend on passivity and daydreams more than most. Reverie is a necessary part of sanity for all of us. As long as a person is chained to a psychotic illness, a doctor might consider that she needs more than the usual amount of room to wander, just as someone with another condition might require extra bed rest. Nudging such a patient into the daily transactional flow of life might give the family hope from seeing their loved one go through the motions of ordinary existence, but it might not serve the patient.

Beyond that, Fleischman is admonishing his profession for

going too far in defining "normal." What right does the DSM task force have to rule that someone who cannot spend eight to ten hours a day in productive activity does not have a genuine role to play in society—as dreamer, lover, artist, visionary? Fleischman's critique opens outward, suggesting that the problems of psychiatry may be rooted in larger arenas: the political system, the whole way of life that we consider normal. "A culture like our own, obsessed with independence and efficiency, will continue to find that injecting cures into schizophrenic patients will make them worse."[12]

In India, Fleischman found schizophrenic patients who, while not receiving the same high levels of psychiatric treatment that they might in the United States, have something that might possibly suit them more. They have families. They are not subdivided into a separate class of society; they spend their days not in alien, fluorescent-lit hospital rooms but "sitting on charpoys in the shade of the earthen walls of their family home, surrounded by the hubbub of joint familial life yet tacitly excused from it. . . ."[13] Fleischman was amazed that this situation seemed to suit everyone concerned—the mentally ill had an accepted place in the flow of life.

Why are there more cases of schizophrenia and depression in the United States today than ever before, even given the many advances in psychiatric treatment? Fleischman does not have a ready answer, but he doesn't exactly give a vote of confidence to the system in which he works. "If I become schizophrenic," he told his colleagues, "mail me to Poona."[14]

4

Storming the Castle

A one-legged Chilean on a diving board. It could be a Zen koan, a quixotic image on which to focus the mind in meditation. It could be a piece of a dream dredged up in the course of psychotherapy ("How do you know he's a Chilean? What does Chile signify to you? What happened to the other leg?") As it happens, it was the start of a renaissance.

The psychospiritual renaissance—the rediscovery of the Jamesian vision—began, appropriately, in New York City, the center of traditional psychoanalysis and psychiatry in the United States. Both professions are ruled by East Coast fiefdoms—the psychiatry departments at Harvard, Columbia, Cornell, Yale, New York University, Mount Sinai School of Medicine, Albert Einstein College of Medicine, and the University of Pittsburgh, as well as the Washington, D.C.–based American Psychiatric Association—that throughout the century remained strictly obedient to the biomedical model. New

York, the home of the New York Psychoanalytic Institute, which continues to disgorge genuine Freudian analysts steeped in the ways of the id and the superego, and of several of the country's major psychiatric training institutions, is the de facto capital of both professions. Next to Vienna, it is probably the city most associated with Freud, godless rationality, and little men with pointy beards and Naugahyde couches.

New York gained its psychoanalytical status as a result of World War II, when hundreds of analysts and psychiatrists fled Europe and many of them ended up there. (Besides displacing Freud, Adler, and other leaders of the profession, the Nazis destroyed Freud's personal library and most other books and centers of study related to the "Jewish science.") Curiously, once established in the United States, psychoanalysis became even more narrow. Against Freud's wishes, the New York Psychoanalytic Society decided in 1927 that in order to be certified in psychoanalysis one had to be a medical doctor. Freud objected that this would "turn psychoanalysis into a mere housemaid of psychiatry," but the American Medical Association supported the move and it became gospel.

One might expect Freud to have encouraged the linking of psychoanalysis and medicine. He opposed it because his vision of psychoanalysis—and that of many of his followers—was so breathtakingly broad. Psychoanalysis had implications, in the words of Ernest Jones, Freud's friend, colleague, and biographer, for "anthropology, mythology, and folklore; the historical evolution of mankind with the various divergent routes this has followed; the upbringing and education of children; the significance of artistic endeavor; the vast field of sociology with a more penetrating estimate of the various social institutions, such as marriage, law, religion, and perhaps even government."[1] In short, psychoanalysis was going to change the world, over and over again. To limit its practice to medical doctors would mean that specialists in these other fields would not be able to put this powerful new tool to full use. Freud's dream (never realized) was for specialized colleges to be established for the teaching of psychoanalysis; students would take courses in science, mythology, and great literature, as well as receive analytical training.

Another consequence of the war, which narrowed the parameters of the field in subtler ways, had to do with language. With the shift from Germany and Austria to the United States, the lingua franca of psychology changed from German to English. As Bruno Bettelheim charted in his 1982 book *Freud and Man's Soul*, Freud was systematically misrepresented in English. While he may have been guilty of reductionist thinking, Freud did not oversimplify the workings of the human psyche. He deliberately used the word *seele*, soul, throughout his writings when he wanted to take his thoughts to the edge of the deepest pools; he was, Bettelheim argued, adopting theological terminology in order to be purposely imprecise, to refer to "the ambiguity of the psyche itself, which reflects many different, warring levels of consciousness simultaneously." In English, however, *seele* became "mind" and "mental life"—just one example of the sanitizing and tidying process that Freud's works went through in translation in order to make them more palatable to the medical establishment. It apparently succeeded, and in the process psychoanalysis moved that much further from the territory that a term like *soul* suggests.

New York became the center, then, of a decidedly narrow and scientifically oriented profession. So it is perhaps appropriately ironic that, flowing out of the 1960s, New York also became the breeding ground for the psychospiritual renaissance. This new wave began not with learned symposia or panels of graybearded experts debating the question, but with a young man from South America balancing himself on five toes high above a swimming pool. His name was Tomás Agosin. He wasn't famous, but when he died in 1991 at the age of forty-three, a memorial service was held at the United Nations, and busloads of people from all walks of life, city powerbrokers to homeless drug addicts, attended, wept, and offered testimonials to how he had changed their lives.

He had been born into a wealthy Jewish family in Chile; as a child he developed cancer and had to have one leg amputated. Death became a palpable presence for him, but illness and the hovering sense of impermanence lightened him, made him freer in his feelings than most teenage boys are. He made friends easily, and most of these had the strong impression that they were his best friend.

He came to New York to get treatments at the Rusk Institute of Rehabilitation Medicine, and stayed. He attended New York University and became a fixture of the Greenwich Village scene, where he was known for hanging out with beggars as much as with coeds. He approached his studies, his friendships, and the churning downtown scene of the late 1960s with the same combination of delight at the beauty and fascination with the darkness. He reveled in complexity; he was an Ingmar Bergman fanatic.

Agosin graduated from NYU and was accepted to study medicine at Albert Einstein College of Medicine. It was in 1970, early in his first year at Einstein, that he established a friendship that would in time change a generation of psychotherapeutic professionals.

Swimming was good physical therapy, but Agosin had to go one step beyond and execute dives—difficult dives—at the pool at the nurses' residence at Jacobi Hospital in the Bronx, which was open to med students. Peter Cohen, another first-year student, was entering the pool area just as the one-legged Agosin had positioned himself at the end of the diving board.

Had he come on such a sight in later years, when he was steeped in spiritual and psychotherapeutic ways of knowing, in symbolism and parabolic meanings, Cohen might have stopped and observed and appreciated. Instead, he blurted out, "What the hell's that guy doing up there?"

Whereupon Agosin replied, "A one and a half," and executed it.

The two became friends. Today Peter Cohen is one of the leaders of the psychospiritual movement. In 1970, he was a Jewish guy from Schenectady who in his first semester at medical school was having a miserable time: "I was going to be an M.D., but I passed out at the sight of blood. They said, 'You'll get over it,' but I didn't. Basically, I was very unhappy. I had all these issues from my past that I hadn't dealt with at all, I'd just buried them, and now that I was in this intense environment they were overwhelming me."

Cohen was intrigued by his friend. "We were the same age, but he wasn't like anyone else. The accent, the missing leg, the air of wisdom. He had friends on all different levels of society. He'd hang out with people who lived in the subway, who he knew from the treatment program, but his girlfriend was a Pan Am stewardess. He charmed me the way he charmed everyone."

Agosin saw that his friend was hurting. "We'll get you a psychologist," he told him. He also introduced Cohen to his spiritual path. Agosin was a member of Cafh, a vaguely esoteric, nondoctrinaire spiritual order that began in Buenos Aires in the 1930s and was one of several similar forms of spirituality that jumped from South America to the United States during the 1960s, at the same time that Transcendental Meditation and various practices from the East were gaining a foothold. Thanks to Agosin, Cohen started psychotherapy and a spiritual pursuit in the same month; shortly thereafter he took a leave of absence from medical school. Cohen liked the loose fit of Cafh and the lack of emphasis on a deity, but he didn't feel comfortable telling his therapist, a Freudian analyst from the New York Psychoanalytic Institute, about it. In his therapy he began to look at himself as if through someone else's eyes. He saw a Jewish kid who was ashamed of his Jewishness, who had gone to Princeton at a time when Waspishness and atheism were de rigueur.

Cohen never went back to medical school but became a psychologist instead. Today he has a private psychotherapy practice just down the road from the Princeton campus and another office in Brooklyn. But he has become influential among his colleagues not so much for his practice as for his extracurricular work, which began with Agosin.

Agosin cruised through medical school, became a psychiatrist, and advanced quickly to become associate director of residency training at Albert Einstein. He made a name for himself as an administrator and teacher but especially in his clinical work. Unlike virtually all psychiatrists in the 1970s and 1980s, he carried his spiritual sensibility right into the clinical setting. The Group for the Advancement of Psychiatry stated the prevailing wisdom in 1976 when it defined religious belief as "borderline psychosis" and "a regression, an escape, a projection upon the world of a primitive infantile state."[2]

But Cafh encourages its followers to see the mystical, the transcendent, the wondrous in everyday life, and Agosin brought this wide-eyed awareness right into his clinical practice. It was instantly noticeable to patients. Within a short time patients with psychospiritual ailments began to seek him out, and Agosin developed a way of dealing with a variety of mental problems, from psychosis to depression, that relied on his spiritual sensibility and, just as important, on his reading of Jung.

Of the handful of major psychiatrists and psychoanalysts

who from the time of William James took religious experience seriously and tried in some way to include it in their models of the psyche, Jung has surely been the most influential. He was the boldest in his efforts to pull and stretch psychological theory until it could wrap itself around myth and spirit. The terminology Jung created in the process has become as much a part of pop culture as Freud's: persona, collective unconscious, archetype, animus, and anima. This entire Jungian vocabulary fits into the man's vision of the limitlessness of psychology as it bleeds across the individual-biological boundary and into the arcing sky of spirit.

Jung's way of allowing for that bleeding of individual psyche into world spirit was by going down deep: at the inner core of the individual personality lies the collective unconscious, the pool of archetypes with which the primordial parts of our mind organize the world and so make it meaningful. Several archetypes form the cluster called the ego, the seemingly autonomous individual: me. But behind the ego, and at the very core of the personality, lies the archetype that Jung named (somewhat confusingly) the Self: the part of the individual psyche that feels a connection with the universe. The Self, according to Agosin, "is the archetype of totality and wholeness. . . . It is the God-within."[3] Jung believed that man is "naturally religious" and that the Self is the source of religiosity.

Jung's rise in popularity mirrored Freud's decline, but that trend may be ending. Recent biographies highlight the dark shadow of Jung's own psyche: his racism, his anti-Semitism, his Nazi sympathies (the Nazis gave him the task, which he seems to have pursued, of attempting to extract "Aryan psychology" from "Jewish psychology"). And, interestingly, while Jung has become the godfather of the new spirituality in America, an important influence on everything from Joseph Campbell's mythological theories to Thomas Moore's psychospiritual reflections to the plot of the mystical best-seller *The Celestine Prophecy*, throughout his writings Jung lays down a caveat: all he is doing is psychology, describing what he has observed from clinical work; he makes no claims that there actually *is* such a thing as transcendence, only that we have a chunk of our psyche that seems to be made for transcendence. Throughout his career he waffled when pressed to say whether or not he believed in God.

Jungians today take pains to point out that the man's personal failings do not erase his professional achievements. Agosin believed that Jung was "the first modern psychoanalytic thinker who integrated psyche and spirit."[4]

Like Jung, Agosin believed that religion, the "quest for wholeness," is at the root of many major mental illnesses, and he treated patients accordingly. A woman came to see him suffering from severe depression. She was not religious; her only passion was for food, and she was grossly overweight. Over the course of the therapy, however, she developed a new, intense passion for Agosin, a particularly acute form of the psychotherapeutic transference. She expressed her love for him overtly and virtually demanded that they have an affair. After he refused, she came back in the next session and reported a dream she had had:

"You were crucified as Jesus Christ. You were almost naked on the cross. I was kneeling at your feet and had a bowl in my hands, collecting your blood and drinking it."[5]

A Freudian analyst might have seen the image of the crucified therapist as representing her rage at Agosin for rejecting her, and beneath that the subconscious presence of the woman's father, who had been both successful and loving but who had eventually abandoned his family, causing in her a life-long wound.

But Agosin took the symbolism deeper still. The woman's

problem, he believed, had to do with the relationship between the ego and the Self, the "God-within." In normal, healthy consciousness, according to the Jungian model, the ego and the Self are connected but separate, so that one has an everyday awareness of oneself as a distinct person but also has the capacity to feel wonder, awe, and transcendent unity. If there is no contact between the ego and the Self, however, a person feels unconnected to others, to nature, to God; the result, in clinical terms, is depression.

Such a person may, if deeply moved, locate the Self externally—in a cause or another person. "My understanding was that she had projected the Self onto me, and I was carrying the numinosity in her life," Agosin wrote. Jung saw Jesus Christ as the psychological symbol of the Self in the Western world. If the Self is our innate awareness of our own participation in divinity, Christ is the literalization of that awareness—God-made-flesh, or the human being divinified. The early Christian leaders responsible for the gospels provided for this awareness to be transferred to and incorporated in each believer in the most literal way. True life only began with the consumption of Christ's flesh and blood:

> [U]nless you eat the flesh of the Son of Man and drink his blood, you have no life in you. Those who eat my flesh and drink my blood have eternal life, and I will raise them up on the last day; for my flesh is true food and my blood is true drink. Those who eat my flesh and drink my blood abide in me, and I in them. Just as the living Father sent me, and I live because of the Father, so whoever eats me will live because of me.[6]

"Her erotic longings for me were a desire to connect with and feel nurtured by the Self," Agosin wrote. Blood represents the essence of life: "The dream was telling her to drink of her Self so as to rejuvenate her psychic life," or, in other words, "to establish a connection to something meaningful and transcendent in her life."

Agosin discussed his interpretation of the dream with the woman; the result was a remarkable change beginning in the next session. The woman gushed forth with a new love for her parents. For the first time she saw them as struggling, imperfect beings. She felt filled with forgiveness and understanding of their hardships. She stopped overeating and lost weight. She felt a new love for her own family. It was, Agosin decided, a promising beginning.

Agosin's analysis of the treatment was in terms of Jungian archetypes: "Contact with the Self transforms the state of the ego. From anger, depression, emptiness, and a clinging love, to forgiveness, gratitude, and expansive love." In common with people who experience deep religious feelings, the woman had lost the need to attend and feed and devote energy to shoring up her self, and instead felt a rush of outward energy and, with it, love for others.

Another patient came to Agosin with the complaint that he had been hospitalized five times in three years when in a psychotic state, which he described as "feeling he was God—a very beautiful, intense, and extraordinary experience." In this state the man felt "energy exploding all around him" but also that he had "taken all the suffering of the world" and was overwhelmed by the burden. His last hospitalization came after transit police found him walking on the subway tracks; the man thought he could stop the train with his thoughts. He was worried about himself, but also believed the episodes were somehow important.

Agosin told him something no doctor had ever dared to: "I told him that I understood that those times were the most precious and meaningful moments in his life." Tears came into the man's eyes.

This man's situation was the opposite of the woman's, one in which the ego is lost in the Self, drowning in the Self. Agosin talked with his patient about "the need to make his ego stronger so that it would not be totally taken over by the Self " and treated the man with a combination of psychotherapy and medication. Having his experience credited as a spiritual event, as "ecstatic suffering," enabled the man to accept that the other part of his life, the material daily routine, was also important and needed to be maintained, and convinced him that he should keep taking the medicine.

The connection between psychosis and mysticism became an important part of Agosin's work and outlook. He came into contact with David Lukoff's work on the intersection of the two states, and used Lukoff's analysis of the differences and similarities of the two as well as his own reading of Jung to build his perspective. Agosin concluded that the psychotic and the genuine mystic have the same psychological setup, in which the ego has become lost in the Self, which causes both to feel a profound and important union of the individual identity with something larger. But Agosin also believed that there were crucial differences between the two states. One of the tip-offs to psychotic delusion, which has been known since William James's time, is grandiosity*: a mystic is humbled by his experience, a psychotic inflated.

While Agosin's career was progressing, Peter Cohen had become so dedicated to his own spiritual undertaking, and at the same time so troubled by his profession's whitewashing of

---

*James divided this psychotic grandiosity into two forms, based on personality type. An extroverted psychotic grandiosity he termed fanaticism, and for the introverted form, which causes one to dwell on God's particular love for oneself, to the exclusion of all else, James coined the refreshingly nonclinical term "theopathic absorption."

religion, that he devoted his doctoral dissertation to a study of religiously committed psychological clinicians. Pursuing both a spiritual life and a psychotherapeutic training was like leading a double life; he wanted to understand how older colleagues who were also deeply religious managed to integrate the two. What he discovered was that for the most part they didn't; they didn't talk about their spirituality to colleagues, and didn't try to bring the two parts of themselves together. Cohen was not sure that integration was possible, but he felt uncomfortable with the dichotomy in his life. Agosin did, too, and one day in 1987 he suggested they deal with the issue directly and publicly by confronting their colleagues. Together with a Buddhist psychotherapist named Mark Finn, they decided to do a presentation on psychotherapy and spirituality at the Cafh meeting space on the Upper West Side of Manhattan.

More than a decade later, this hardly seems a radical notion, but at the time it was risky. The institutional disdain of religion was so deep that they actually had dreams of being laughed out of the profession.

Their fears were misplaced. So many psychotherapists showed up for the presentation that the small space couldn't hold them all, so they had to run the program twice. "People got in touch with me afterward," Cohen said. "It turned out they were all on paths of their own. They were practicing yoga or were Buddhists or were Jewish or Catholic or whatever, and they didn't talk about it with their colleagues—ironic, because of course therapists are supposed to be able to explore uncomfortable subjects. Suddenly they felt they could discuss this without making fun of it. It was like the days when people would make fun of gays in the locker room—an apt analogy because it was very much like coming out of the closet."

That presentation became the seed for a movement. Since 1980 Albert Einstein College of Medicine has sponsored a summer seminar series in Massachusetts for psychotherapeutic professionals from around the country, called the Cape Cod Institute. The Institute, being a summer school, has a laid-back feel, but it is also serious and mainstream. The top of the profession is featured, and special seminars cover such topics as gestalt therapy and "neurodevelopmental variation in childhood and adolescence." After doing one or two more of their "Psychotherapy and the Spirit" presentations, Agosin and his colleagues, who were now joined by Boston College religion professor John McDargh, won an invitation to lead one of the Cape Cod seminars. "Overnight we went from small-time gigs to playing the main event," Cohen said. They approached the event with all the studiousness of a cadre of academicians; in jackets and ties, they took turns reading carefully prepared twenty-page papers that laid out arguments and theories suggesting that there was a home for spirituality in the profession. The response was overwhelming. "Psychotherapy and Spirituality" won the highest ratings of any program ever offered at the Institute. In the past, no seminar had ever been repeated, but Agosin and his mates were asked back a second time the following summer. Then, a third time. Agosin was especially emboldened. He gave major presentations at the annual meeting of the APA on the overlap of psychological and spiritual concerns. All of them could sense that they were riding the beginnings of a wave, that a real change was happening in the profession.

And then everything seemed to fall apart. In the summer of 1991, while vacationing in Martha's Vineyard, Agosin developed an embolism that lodged in his pulmonary artery. He slipped into a coma and never emerged from it. Death, which had hovered around him since childhood, giving him such a taste for life, finally closed its transaction. Cohen, Finn, and the many colleagues who had become close with them through the brief period in which their psychospiritual movement had come to life, were stunned. Agosin had been the undisputed leader; now it was assumed that the roadshow would close.

But after grieving for a time Cohen and Finn decided not to let it end. They had been invited back to the Cape for a third time; they would go on again, as a tribute to their mentor. In the past they had felt a deficiency in the program because there was no female presence, so as a replacement for Agosin they recruited one of his former students, Fredrica Halligan, who was now assistant director of Fordham University's Counseling Center, and presented themselves as the Agosin Group. Besides providing a female sensibility Halligan also shared Agosin's Jungian perspective, and so brought some continuity.

The Agosin Group has been a feature of the Cape Cod Institute ever since. Hundreds of psychologists, psychiatrists, and others in the mental health professions have participated in it and come away with the once outrageous-seeming notion that it was permissible to develop a spiritual attunement alongside one's clinical, intellectual demeanor, and that encouraging a patient's full emotional development might involve encouraging spiritual development. The lineup of the Cape Cod Institute itself reflects the change that has come over the profession as a whole: the 1998 program included, in addition to the Agosin Group, Herbert Benson presenting recent findings in mind-body medicine, Thomas Moore on "The Soul in Psychotherapy," and psychologist James Spira on "Meditation as Medicine."

Cohen has also continued the program that he and Agosin began at the Cafh Foundation in New York. "Psychotherapy and the Spirit" has run one Saturday a month since 1988, has featured a hugely eclectic group of presenters, and has given more than one thousand clinicians encouragement to develop their own spiritual lives and to encourage their patients to see themselves as something more than hermetically sealed individual selves.

At the time Agosin and Cohen began both groups there were similar gatherings taking place on the West Coast under the aegis of transpersonal psychology, but there was a difference—the people on the West Coast were consciously operating outside the mainstream. By contrast, "We were coming out of the conservative establishment of psychoanalytic thought," Cohen said. "That's why it was new, and that's why we were so scared at first. These people who were coming to see us were the people in the hospitals and the teaching institutions, people in the mainstream. We were storming the castle."

•   •   •

At the same time that he was taking part in Cohen and Agosin's panel, Mark Finn was building another psyche-spirit bridge that would soon become well trodden—between psychoanalysis and Buddhism. Finn grew up in a wealthy Irish-Catholic Boston home, the son of a surgeon who had originally wanted to be a psychoanalyst. "My father was humanistically educated, and in that milieu at that time—a kind of prep school, Ivy League Boston family—religion, meaning Catholicism, just wasn't acceptable. But Buddhism had a sort of respectability." Finn was enamored of both Buddhism and psychoanalysis from early on—"I wanted to be a psychotherapy teacher when I was eighteen"—and began serious practice of Tibetan Buddhism in 1974. As he went through his training in psychology he identified with Erich Fromm, who, a generation after Jung, attempted to align psychoanalysis with Zen Buddhism via his association with the Zen scholar D. T. Suzuki. Fromm was in part reacting to existentialism, which had taken hold in psychoanalysis and philosophy, and to the "spiritual crisis" of the 1950s: "It is the crisis which has been described as 'malaise,' 'ennui,' '*mal du siècle*,' the deadening of life, the automatization of man, his alienation from himself, from his fellow man and from nature," he wrote in the 1960s cult classic *Zen Buddhism and Psychoanalysis*.[7]

Fromm sounds like any godless existentialist scribbling

away in a Parisian café (actually, he was a German who emigrated to America in 1934 and spent most of his years at Michigan State University and Columbia) when he writes that the duty of the authentic individual is "to acknowledge his fundamental aloneness and solitude in a universe indifferent to his fate, to recognize that there is no power transcending him which can solve his problem for him."[8] But then Fromm turns cosmic: "[A]ll human beings are identical. We are all part of One; we are One. This being so, it should not make any difference whom we love."[9]

Fromm could have it both ways—we are lone individuals, but we are spiritually One—by putting religion to work for existentialism; the kind of religion he valued, "humanistic religion," sees "the experience of oneness with the All, based on one's relatedness to the world as it is grasped with thought and with love."[10]

Religion was acceptable to Fromm provided one didn't get too literal about it. Do away with dogma and literalistic ideas of a graybearded Man in the Sky, and, Fromm said, you have the beginnings of a grown-up, twentieth-century religion: "Inasmuch as humanistic religions are theistic, God is a symbol of *man's own powers* which he tries to realize in his life, and is not a symbol of force and domination, having power over man."[11] Fromm anticipated the new spirituality of today when he suggested that true spirituality does not depend on outmoded concepts like God. In the foreword to *Psychoanalysis and Religion* he pointed to a sentence by the Belgian priest and Nobel Peace Prize-winner Georges Henri Pire as best representing his kind of spirituality: "What matters is not the difference between believers and unbelievers, but between those who care and those who do not care."[12]

Fromm identified a similarity between psychoanalysis and the Buddhist worldview. "While psychiatry is concerned with the question of why *some* people become insane," he wrote, "the real question is why *most* people do *not* become insane."[13] Mountains of grief, endless toil, the naked fact of death: why don't we all simply crack under the strain? Mostly, we dodge these lethal bullets by busying ourselves with "compensatory mechanisms"—career and money, getting to the next rung, making it to the next vacation. But "the only fundamental solution which truly overcomes potential insanity is the full, productive response to the world which in its highest form is enlightenment." Enlightenment, of course, is Buddha-speak, but Western Buddhist interpreters, from Fromm to Mark Finn, believe it is translatable into the language of psycho-analysis. The enlightenment of psychoanalysis—"making the unconscious conscious"—comes from peeling away the layers of defense: the subterfuges and distractions. The therapy process is a kind of training, hard work that steels the soul and prepares it to face itself with fewer buffers and distractions. Without this training such a sight *would* lead to insanity. Most schools of Buddhism also lead students through stages of train-ing, in the form of meditation, as a result of which one comes to see oneself stripped of the usual defenses.

In following Fromm into the Buddhism-psychoanalysis nexus, and in doing so in the 1980s, Mark Finn was catching a wave that is still crashing in the psychotherapeutic professions. Why has Buddhism become so acceptable, so fashionable among therapists? "One reason is Buddhism was presented here as a therapy right from the get-go," said Finn. " 'Do you believe in God or not?' was not a relevant question. Believing in God was Freud's believing in the father. Western religions have to grapple with that. Buddhism doesn't."

Mark Epstein, a Harvard-educated Buddhist psychiatrist, the author of the best-selling *Thoughts Without a Thinker*, took part in the first conference that Finn organized. He believes therapists have been drawn to Buddhism as psychology's view of the self has changed. "My basic take on this is that psychoanalysis, through its own method of inquiry into the nature of the self, has come to a place of understanding of the Buddhist view of the self. That's why it's Buddhism, and not Judaism or something else, that's so interesting right now. The method of inquiry of psychoanalysis has shown analysts themselves that it's really hard to put your finger on this thing, the self. The inquiry itself is spiritual—I think there is something spiritual here, in creating this empty space. And through that method these analysts come to that space instead of just falling off the edge and saying there's nothing there but instincts."

Epstein teaches in NYU's popular postdoctoral program in Buddhism and psychoanalysis and is a regular speaker on the topic. Others have taken Buddhism in various directions. One of the hottest innovations in the field is dialectical behavior therapy; Marsha Linehan, its creator, participated in Finn's first conference and relates its insights to Buddhist meditation techniques. The Buddhist magazine *Tricycle* regularly devotes pages to the ins and outs of the Buddhism-psychotherapy linkage.

But none of that existed in 1987, when Finn met a couple of therapists at a Buddhist retreat, they fell to talking, and the idea of a conference emerged. Several months later, four hundred psychotherapeutic professionals and others gathered at Columbia University to witness a first-of-its-kind spectacle. One half of the stage was occupied by a rotating panel of several of the most distinguished and/or provocative figures in psychiatry and psychoanalysis, including R. D. Laing, one of the modern innovators in psychotherapy; John Mack, the Harvard psychiatrist and future promoter of alien abduction; Thomas Szasz, the antipsychiatry psychiatrist; Edward Podvoll, a leading psychiatric innovator at the Naropa Institute; Edward Whitmont, a founding member of the C. G. Jung Institute in

New York; and Paul Fleischman. On the other side, decked out in their resplendent robes, sat several Tibetan lamas, including Jamgon Kongtrul Rinpoche, direct holder of the Karma Kagyu lineage who was revered as a living Buddha. At some point early in the proceedings, as the audience rustled with nervous anticipation and Allen Ginsberg prepared to read a poem, Finn suddenly felt dazed. "I was just two years out of graduate school. It suddenly seemed I had gotten in over my head." His fear was that he had forced a bizarre, artificial linkage between two groups who would have absolutely nothing to say to each other.

Things didn't turn out quite that way, but Finn said the biggest problem with the event was that the lamas "basically just wanted to be lamas—they weren't really interested in psychotherapy." The shrinks, however, dove into the arcana of psychoanalytic theory and Zen. At times the discussion became a shooting match of East-meets-West wisdom. The quintessential moment came after an arcane discussion of the ego and the self and the nature of Zen. "We opened the floor to questions," Finn said, "and a woman stands up and says, 'I don't care about how many Zen masters can fit on the head of a pin. I want to know about shitting and pissing and fucking.' " There was a lot of laughter and nodding of heads; there was general agreement that it was a moment of group self-discovery; *this* was what they should be talking about, the gutsy stuff of real life. But by remaining lamas the lamas trumped everyone else. Khenpo Karthar Rinpoche, the august abbot of Tibetan monasteries in Bhutan and New York, asked, through a translator, what the woman had said. Finn replied directly, with what he was sure the lama would recognize as true Zen wisdom, that she had wanted to know about shitting and pissing and fucking. The translator translated, Rinpoche looked confused, then he said, "But how has she managed up until this point?"

Despite the fact that Finn thought it came off "like a badly organized rock concert," the conference was widely considered a success—mostly because it had happened. A bridge had been built between two formerly separate islands, and people were now walking across it. A rush of academic papers, popular books, and continuing education lectures began. Most surprising to Finn was the reaction he got from the psychoanalytic establishment. "There *was* no reaction. It started to dawn on me the year before, when I brought Jamgon Kongtrul Rinpoche to meet a group of analysts, and they were respectful of his spiritual eminence and genuinely interested in what he had to say. I began to realize that the enemy didn't exist, that we had won the war without realizing it."

The change may have begun at the grass-roots level: ordinary people were receptive to this broadening of the field before most practitioners were. Alcoholics Anonymous and other twelve-step programs, which twine psychological prescriptions around a trunk of spirituality, had been massively popular for years before the psychological profession took serious notice.

One can, in some fashion, chart the popular growth of this hunger by means of a particular case study. When, in 1978, a Connecticut psychiatrist published a self-help book that drew on both psychoanalytic theory and spiritual wisdom, it sold a modest ten thousand copies in its first year. Then, defying publishing norms, its sales doubled the following year, and doubled again, and again, and kept going, until M. Scott Peck's *The Road Less Traveled* became a virtual industry. Peck has credited the book's unprecedented success to AA, which made millions of people comfortable with the idea that spiritual release was an important step to psychological growth, that one's psychological and spiritual selves could be seen as on a continuum rather than as two separate entities. The book, and Peck himself, was largely ignored by the psychiatric profession until its popularity simply commanded attention.

"Through all these years I have received nothing but support for this work," Mark Finn said of his Buddhism-psychoanalysis linkage. Cohen's theory is that "hooking into the spirit" has become perceived as politically correct, so that those traditionally minded psychoanalysts who might oppose it prefer not to go on record doing so. "Also, psychoanalysis, which used to be the big critic of religion, has been on the run, and it is changing its focus entirely, away from autonomy and toward interdependence. And many types of religious experience are compatible with that."

This is not to say that everyone in the psychiatric and psychological establishments actively embraces the movement into spirituality; it is perhaps safer to say that many traditional practitioners who aren't themselves inclined in this direction don't find anything particularly wrong with it, provided it is done responsibly (without proselytizing, for instance) and with respect to the different roles that clergy and psychotherapists play. The closest any of the gatekeepers of the psychiatric profession will come to actual criticism is to question how much real traction the movement has. Benjamin Sadock, coauthor of the *Comprehensive Textbook of Psychiatry*, the leading textbook in the field, said, for instance, that there are no plans to devote more space to religious and spiritual issues in the next edition because "the trends in psychiatry are pharmacological. To that extent, both psychoanalysis and religion are probably diminishing in importance."

But those in the movement do not see these two things—an increased focus on psychiatric medicine and on spiritual concerns—as mutually exclusive. Most see the new generations of psychiatric drugs, which tend to address debilitating symptoms more effectively than earlier ones and with fewer side effects, as enormously helpful for many patients. Moving into the nonrational arena of religion, they argue, does not require them to swear off laboratory research and clinical psychology. The field remains a medical practice, rooted in the rational.

The loudest criticism of the movement has probably come from within the psychospiritual community. Paul Fleischman is one of many spiritually oriented psychiatrists who argue against the idea that the realm of the spirit and the realm of the ego are the same. Jeffrey Rubin, like Finn a Buddhist practitioner, and the author of a book on the Buddhism-therapy alignment, has been critical of the too-easy embrace of an Eastern path. The argument is that Western society has a tendency either to destroy or idealize other cultures, to slaughter the savages or make out that their variety of worship is purer and truer.

In its second year, 1988, the Buddhism and Psychoanalysis conference drew double the audience—eight hundred people—including many more establishment figures. "Suddenly I started to hear all sorts of therapists saying they were Buddhists," Finn said. "Family therapy people came up to me saying *they* were the real Buddhist therapists."

Just when it became clear that he had instigated a minimovement, Finn lost interest. The conferences were an organizational headache, and they involved what he calls "the management of psychospiritual celebrities." Almost overnight, the psyche-spirit movement went from a few people sitting in a room talking to a small industry—one that people were using to advance their careers.

Finn has a florid, jowly face—what you might call an Irish boxer's face; his eyes are slits and he has a tendency to giggle. He comes across like a poet boxer: physical but sensitive. He is chief psychologist at North Central Bronx Hospital and a regular on the lecture circuit. He is still happy to talk to whomever will listen about the East-meets-West possibilities that he has been exploring all these years, but he has little interest in the politics of it. "This has all gotten a little public for me. I'm a countercultural guy at heart."

Finn ran a few more conferences, but he scaled them down and moved them out of Manhattan to the hamlet of Woodstock, New York. "I'm traveling lighter than I did a few years ago," he said. "My definitions of both Buddhism and psychotherapy have softened." He has decided that questions about the theory behind each discipline, how they can be combined and where they overlap are not so important to him after all. After all, it is experience, living in the moment, that matters. "The Woodstock gatherings were more my style, more conversational. My favorite moment was the time we rented a small restaurant and just talked over dinner. Allen Ginsberg was a huge help to us through all the conferences, and at that one he sang William Blake's *Songs of Experience* while we ate. Eating dinner with all these interesting people, listening to Ginsberg chant 'Tyger Tyger.' That was a really nice moment."

•   •   •

As prescient and daring as they have been, Agosin, Cohen, and Finn have worked their psyche-spirit theme in a rather small and sheltered setting, the clubbish world of professional psychology. Their efforts in East Coast establishment circles through the 1980s and those of the transpersonal crowd on the West Coast were like two small fires that grew steadily brighter. At some point the heat became intense enough for the blaze to engulf a wider area. It just needed the right person to come along and spread it.

That person is David Larson. Larson has taken the Jamesian notion that religion and psychology are not distinct but blend into one another—that private religious experience cannot be divorced from science (or, in James's words, "The axis of reality runs solely through the egotistic places")—and gone wide with it. Larson has spread the fire from psychology and psychiatry into medicine as a whole, and has stoked the flames in the mass media and for a receptive public. He has brought his message—that the medical establishment has long ignored religion as a factor in health, though studies now show it has an overwhelmingly positive effect—to the American Association of Medical Colleges, the American Psychiatric Association, bioethics seminars, and various mind-body conferences. He has elaborated on it for the benefit of *Good Morning America, ABC World News Tonight, CBS Evening News, NBC Nightly News,* MSNBC, CNN, *Time, Newsweek, USA Today, The New York Times, The Washington Post, Psychology Today, Reader's Digest, Utne Reader,* the *Christian Science Monitor,* and the *Journal of the American Medical Association.* He has probably done more than any other single person to investigate and publicize the damage caused by society's following the narrow, Freudian path to medical wisdom. His timing has been impeccable: doctors of all stripes are now touching their patients, talking about the spiritual dimensions of healing, even praying with patients.

Larson is a psychiatrist and an epidemiologist with adjunct professorships at Duke University Medical Center, Northwestern University Medical School, and the Uniformed Services University of the Health Sciences. For ten years he was a senior researcher at the National Institutes of Health. He is a part of the American medical establishment, but his beginnings were humble: "I grew up on AFDC. My father died when I was very young, and I was always pretty skinny. We never had many Christmas presents. When you're poor, God can become an important thing, and it was for me."

Larson's background doesn't fit the East Coast liberal, hippie-intellectual mold of Cohen and Finn. He never took up with an esoteric Eastern path. Jesus has always been The Way for him—Jesus and Medicine. The two things were never incompatible to Larson, but in medical school he was struck by a glaring irony: religion was ignored in medical studies, but among the patients he saw in his rounds faith was clearly vitally important. While getting his master's in public health at Northwestern University, he did his thesis on blood pressure and religion and found that people who attended church regularly had lower blood pressure than nonchurchgoers. He encountered a certain amount of suspicion and friction in trying to get the work published (he likes to characterize the study of religion and health as an "anti-tenure track") but it only made him more convinced than ever that religion was "the forgotten factor" in health care, and he determined that this would be his life's work. In 1991 he founded the National Institute for Healthcare Research, a nonprofit clearinghouse for research into the relationship between spirituality and health. The principal funder of NIHR is the John Templeton Foundation, whose eponymous founder made a vast fortune in mutual funds before retiring in 1992 to become the leading philanthropist supporting science-religion causes. (Larson said NIHR has several other benefactors, but "they don't want to be known—they're afraid they'll be accused of brainwashing people into being religious.")

NIHR organizes conferences and sponsors research. In 1997 it bestowed the first John Templeton Awards to eighteen medical schools to start courses on religion for physicians-in-training. "They aren't courses in world religions," Larson hastens to note, "but in, for example, how a Hindu might look at death and dying. The idea is for doctors to appreciate how different cultures view such things." The Pennsylvania State College of Medicine, for one example, now teaches a "Religion and Health" course, in which medical students have to do a spiritual autobiography. In 1998, seven medical schools won the first Templeton Awards specifically intended for psychiatry residency training. A total of three medical schools were teaching such courses in 1994; today Larson estimates that there are about fifty.

Larson is a networking machine. Names fly from him—of medical school deans, psychiatry department heads, hospital administrators, legislators—along with minibios, crisscrossing threads of information tying them to yet other names, and the threads weaving together into the fabric of the American medical establishment. He is also a geyser of statistics: 80 percent of Americans believe that God and/or prayer can help them recover from an illness, but only 10 percent of physicians ask about their patients' religious beliefs. Nonchurchgoers are four times more likely to commit suicide than churchgoers. Forty-five percent of participants in a religious program for heroin addiction were clean a year later, while only 5 percent of those in a nonreligious program were. Eighty-four percent of psychiatric studies involving religion found a positive correlation between religion and health. Clinical psychologists are more than four times as likely to be atheists as the average American.

Larson also chronicles health-spirituality correlations of every type: meditation reduces serum cholesterol levels; religious belief lowers pain levels in cancer patients; more religious people than nonreligious people survive cardiac surgery; there is a correlation between weekly church attendance and lower rates of heart disease and emphysema; in a study involving cardiac patients, those who received intercessory prayer (someone else praying for the patient's recovery) had fewer cases of heart failure, cardiopulmonary arrest, and pneumonia.

Larson and coauthors Jeffrey Levin and Christina Puchalski summarized all of this in ungainly medicalese in a 1997 article in the *Journal of the American Medical Association*: "Systematic reviews and meta-analyses quantitatively confirm that religious involvement is an epidemiologically protective factor."[14] Translation: God is good for your health.

Larson has watched with satisfaction as the interest in tackling religious experience with the tools of science has crept into psychiatry, gerontology, and psychopharmacology. But while he tries hard to convince experts in a variety of fields to take his religion crusade seriously, he seems to go out of his way *not* to involve another important group.

Few people in organized religion seem to know of his efforts, which is just fine with Larson: "I tend not to work with theologians. We're dealing with religion here, but I don't want theologians just now." In his extensive media contacts he deals much more with science and health editors than with religion editors. The fact is he's sensitive to charges that this effort to get people to bring religion and medicine closer together is in fact a subtle form of evangelism. For this same reason Larson labors mightily to get medical people of every stripe into his tent. In 1997 he organized his broadest conference to date, "Scientific Progress in Spirituality," which brought together major figures in psychiatry, social work, psychopharmacology, internal medicine, and sociology, and specialists in addiction, gerontology, and family medicine. "These are not choir members," he insists. "They were suspicious about this at first, but they agreed it had to be looked at." Larson brought them around by voicing their suspicions: "You're afraid this is a religious fundamentalist plot, something like creation science. Well, I think we elites make a mistake when we say, 'It's religion, don't touch it or we'll become leprous.' It's precisely when we do that that it gets unregulated, fundamentalistic."

The reports the conference issued advised sweeping renovations of the medical establishment. They struggled with definitions of religion and spirituality, wrangled over how best to measure them, examined built-in problems with studying the spiritual (How do you identify a nonspiritual control group?), and pointed out structural problems (Will the government pull funding from a study that contains a religious variable on the grounds that it violates the separation of church and state?). They created a "taxonomy of religious/spiritual interventions" that includes forgiveness, release, ritual, and prayer, and suggested that such things be studied the way science studies the effects of particular drugs. They reviewed neuroscientific research into spiritual experiences and suggested guidelines for new research. They went so far as to advocate "neuroscientific investigations into drug-induced spiritual states," which they say "may provide important information for those clinical investigators developing religious or spiritual interventions, and may even allow them to 'fine-tune' such interventions, particularly in the domains of alcohol and drug problems."[15]

One of Larson's most highly publicized sets of statistics concerns prayer. Gallup surveys have found that 77 percent of patients say they would like their doctors to consider their spiritual needs as part of their treatment, and an astonishing 48 percent of patients would like their doctors to pray with them. Larson pushed these statistics in his media venues; he allied himself with Larry Dossey, the physician who brought intercessory prayer to national attention with his best-selling book *Healing Words: The Power of Prayer and the Practice of Medicine*. The subject received a great deal of media attention in the mid-1990s, which seemed to poke a modest hole in the stiff wall of reserve that M.D.'s maintain. In some parts of the country, interns are now accompanying chaplains on their hospital rounds, plugging themselves into their patients' spiritual lives in ways that until recently would have been unthinkable.

In a 1996 mind-body conference in Boston called "Spirituality and Healing in Medicine," sponsored by Harvard Medical School (itself something of a milestone), Larson shared the stage with George Gallup Jr., Dr. Herbert Benson, whose "relaxation response" technique brought meditation into the medical world in the 1970s, Dr. Timothy Johnson, the ABC News medical correspondent, and Dossey. Together this panel presented the gospel of spiritualized medicine to an audience of nearly one thousand physicians, psychologists, nurses, and other practitioners. The conference has since become an annual event. In summarizing what he took to be an incontrovertible rush of statistics proving that religion helps people, psychologically and physically, Gallup concluded—in language that sounds more natural for a pulpited minister than the nation's most respected pollster—that "the burden of proof rests on those who would *deny* that God is active."

In concluding his Gifford Lecture, William James made almost the same statement to his audience: "The uses of religion, its uses to the individual who has it, and the uses of the individual himself to the world, are the best arguments that truth is in it."[16] In both of these statements you have a pragmatist's—a scientist's and a pollster's—affirmation of faith. Our data suggests that God exists. What kind of God? The kind, at the very least, that yields results, in both body and mind. William James is back among us.

5

The Don Quixote
of Westchester

[H]e often found passages like "the reason of
the unreason with which my reason is afflicted
so weakens my reason that with reason I mur-
mur at your beauty"; *or again,* "the high heav-
ens, that of your divinity divinely fortify you
with the stars, render you deserving of the
desert your greatness deserves." *Over conceits
of this sort the poor gentleman lost his wits.*

—CERVANTES, *Don Quixote*

It was the spring of 1973, and the sun was shining in the
medieval streets of Barcelona's Gothic Quarter. Neil Wolf,
an exchange student from White Plains, New York, had
recently enrolled at the University of Barcelona. He was taking
a full slate of courses—Spanish history, art, and culture, as well
as intensive language courses—and spending his free time
roaming the ancient alleyways, stopping to sip coffee in tiny
cafés. In the evening he took his meals at the university cafete-
ria then went for walks along the tree-lined sward called the
Rambla. Westchester County was nothing like this. Barcelona
was glorious, like living in a dream.

But the dream turned. Spain's autoworkers went on strike
against the economic policies of Francisco Franco; when the
students joined them on the picket lines the university shut
down. With riots going on in the streets, Neil sat in his tiny

room, sweating and poring over his books. The year-end exams would be given on schedule, and he would have to prepare for them on his own, in a foreign language, without the help of teachers or classes. If he failed, he would throw a year of his life away.

One night, as the stress reached a peak, he had an actual dream, a nightmare from which he never awoke. It had something to do with a girl he had recently met; strange voices were commanding him. He sat up in bed, terrified, and shivering with relief that it was only a dream. But the voices continued. After a while he determined that it was one voice: his. "I started to hear myself thinking out loud, which, let me tell you, is pretty frightening. Then it progressed, and I thought I was listening to God. Basically, I thought I was the Messiah. You actually hear these voices. They really are coming from outside."

The voice told him that General Franco was going to die and there would be a revolution. His job was to get to a location in the south of Spain and catch a submarine to some undisclosed location. He obeyed orders: he stole a truck and set out across the Spanish countryside. "It was like an adventure, like a delusional form of a Hemingway story." Even more, it was like *Don Quixote*, which Neil had been reading in Spanish:

> In short, his wits being quite gone, he hit upon the strangest notion that every madman in this world hit upon, and that was that he fancied it was right and requisite, as well as for the support of his own honor as for the service of his country, that he should make a knight-errant of himself, roaming the world over in full armor and on horseback in quest of adventures.[1]

"Don Quixote was on a mission," Neil said. "I figured I was a man on a mission, too." He made it as far as Valencia, two hundred miles from Barcelona, before the police stopped him. "I still didn't get it. I thought they were going to lead me to the secret headquarters." Instead, he wound up in jail and then in a mental hospital, before his parents came to bring him back home.

Today Neil is middle-aged, unemployed, and living with his mother in an apartment in White Plains. His ambition of becoming an international businessman has long since evaporated. His diagnosis is schizoaffective disorder. He has been hospitalized forty times since the onset of the illness in Barcelona, often after similar delusional journeys.

Neil's episodes begin with a manic talkativeness, and in this state he talks himself into taking a mental adventure. "I trick my mind into believing there's something else up on another level, and I go higher and higher, until I'm God." As with many people with psychosis, Neil describes the state as blissful. "I've never been as happy as when I've been psychotic. It's like taking drugs. I've taken psychedelics, and I can tell you psychosis is much better. The sheer joy—you think you're the smartest and most powerful man in the world."

But Neil isn't interested in following the course of Joshua Beil and the New Psychotics, who want to explore the opening onto another, spiritual plane that they believe the psychosis gave them. Psychosis hasn't been a brief fling for Neil but a way of life. "I don't want to get into that way of thinking. I'm too old to go back there again. I can't afford the hospitalization. This illness ruined my life. I was going to have a job and a family, you know." Neil does equate the illness with "having a mystical experience—it's like knowing God," but he also points out that the direct experience of God can be terrifying, life-shattering, as well as wondrous. "Psychosis is the greatest joy of my life, and also the worst hell you can imagine."

The problem was that for a long time he kept returning to

the psychosis. He would convince himself to stop taking his medication, to ride the high just one more time. And then he would crash again. Forty hospitalizations, forty adventures in heaven and hell, however, had worn him down. He wanted it to be over. "That's where Dr. Stern has helped me so much. He changed everything, he got me out of that cycle. Imagine a doctor who teaches you how to pray."

Tony Stern, Neil's psychiatrist, goes further than most of his spiritually minded colleagues. He believes in the importance of drugs, but he also believes in the power of prayer, and while in fact he does not actually teach patients to pray, he will in some cases encourage prayer as part of the treatment. What is perhaps even more radical, he believes that psychotherapy itself is a sacred undertaking. In the late 1980s, while doing his residency at New York Hospital–Cornell Medical Center, Stern took part in Agosin and Cohen's first psychotherapy and spirituality gatherings, and he was in the audience at Mark Finn's Buddhism and Psychoanalysis conference. He represents one direction that the psyche-spirit movement has taken since then.

Stern was one of those who found in Tomás Agosin a model of a soulful psychiatrist, but as he progressed on both professional and spiritual tracks, Stern leaned not in the direction of Jung, as Agosin did, but of Martin Buber, the towering Austrian-Jewish intellectual.

In 1952 Buber had such popular renown he appeared at Carnegie Hall. He was not a psychologist but a philosopher and scholar of Judaism who at midcentury became influential among those who wanted to save the psychological worldview from the chill and narrowness of Freud and the biomedical approach. Buber's contributions to rehumanizing psychology were rooted in the mystical teachings of Hasidic Judaism but also had a modern existentialist sensibility. In the materialist view of life we are all alone in an unfeeling, unconscious universe, bumping into "others" like so many molecules colliding in a petri dish. Some of these others are people, but much of the time we don't act as though they are. Our way of dealing with other people is often "I-It"—they are mere things to us. But when we engage in true interaction, deep interaction, in which we care and empathize, in which we open ourselves up to the other person as a true individual, we enter the spiritual realm. This is the "I-Thou" realm.

Dialogue is a sacred act for Buber. Where both Freud and Jung grounded their work in individual consciousness, Buber believed that the individual is only completed in dialogue. In the interaction between an I and a Thou, a new consciousness is discovered, which extends beyond each individual's. Dialogue is more than talking: it is the flow of real communication that makes this new consciousness happen. In fact, Buber insisted that dialogue can happen without anyone uttering a word: "Such simple happenings can be part of it as, for instance, when two strangers exchange glances in a crowded streetcar, at once to sink back again into the convenient state of wishing to know nothing about each other."[2] I-Thou can even take place between opponents, provided that in the intensity of their competition they recognize one another as full human beings rather than mere objects to be overcome. The sacred act of dialogue can occur between such noble enemies whatever the contest—"even if it is no more than a boxing match."[3] Developing this full form of communication, Buber says, is the true path to God. Through meeting each other, we meet God.

I-It, by contrast, is the relationship in which science takes place—it is, literally, the objective stance, in which an external object is recognized and studied. I-It is also the realm of practical living: if you stood around acknowledging the Thou-ness of the sidewalk, you would never get anywhere. I-It is necessary, but it is only one part of being fully human. The individual self, the basis of traditional psychology, is not the point for Buber, any more than it is in the Hebrew Bible, which describes an approach to life and God rooted in community. We become meaningful through our participation in the project of humanity.

Buber's ideas—above all his insistence that the stuff of religion should not be separated from all other human endeavors—rolled like life-giving thunderclouds through the intellectual landscape of the mid-twentieth century, affecting the work of anthropologists, political scientists, and literary critics. But as the center of gravity in the psychotherapeutic professions shifted toward pharmacology, Buber's major insight—that communication between two people, of which psychotherapy is one type, is a holy undertaking—lost influence.

Tony Stern has chaired four national workshops on Buber's philosophy at the annual meetings of the American Psychiatric Association. He is a protégé of the eminent Buber scholar Maurice Friedman. As a speaker and author, Stern is one of the most vigorous, radical, outspoken, and at the same time subtle proponents of psychiatry's embrace of spirituality. He is one of those people who listen to what you say with such focus and intensity that it makes you wonder how much others take in; his face, which reddens easily, changes tones with the slightest alteration in your story. When he talks, it is usually long and energetically; his stories tend to wind around so that you have forgotten the simple question you asked, but he hasn't, and suddenly, like pulling a car up to the place you had forgotten you were looking for, you arrive, he has answered your question, and shown you that the matter is far more complex than you thought.

This intense involvement in the act of conversing derives,

in part, from Stern's reverence for Buber. "Buber talked about the 'between' realm that exists when two people are together, how there is an actual spiritual reality there. It's something very difficult to put in words, but it is vital to psychotherapy and psychiatry. Buber helps us understand the truth of Jesus' comment, 'When two or three are gathered in my name, I am there.' That's what is so unfortunate about much of psychiatry today. Psychiatrists now have less and less therapy training. The pharmacological is important, don't get me wrong, but when you start to think that *talk* is obsolete, you're in big trouble."

This is not to equate the I-Thou therapist-patient relationship with love or empathy, at least not as they are usually defined. "I and Thou is as much about recognizing the other truly as another as it is about recognizing the absolute common ground. It underscores the fullness of the terms love and empathy by embracing the paradox of joining and distance." Another way of explaining it is in terms of the psychotherapeutic transference, the projection of the patient's thoughts and feelings onto the therapist. At some point in the course of therapy, the patient often comes to idealize the therapist. Neil Wolf once said that he "thinks the world of Dr. Stern" and "loves him like a brother." At other points, internal turmoil is foisted outward. "There was a time when Neil was in a bad state and I had to hospitalize him," Stern said. "He didn't want to see me again. But for him to readjust and learn to trust me again after I had so fully opposed him was an important part of therapy. Only agreeing with each other wouldn't lead anywhere real."

The more serious a patient's mental illness, the more important most psychiatrists, including Stern, believe is the interplay of psychiatry's two basic tools: talk and drugs. Working with a mobile crisis team in Westchester County, New York, and with a drug rehabilitation program in the Bronx puts Stern in touch with many seriously disturbed people. If anything, his views on the relationship between psychosis and mysticism are even more radical than Tomás Agosin's or David Lukoff's. Where both of them believe there are important differences between the two states, Stern isn't so sure. "When you're a clinician you see a lot of psychotic people whose lives are clearly not working, who are completely lost in the chaos of it, but who really are in touch with something. I think there's a fine line between the two conditions, and perhaps the underlying process is the same—so that essentially the question is what you do with it, how you respond to it. If you look at the great mystics, I can't think of one who did not show signs of what today would be considered severe psychosis or manic-depressive illness. We could say that the 'illness' of these mystics served as a spiritual death and rebirth experience, but that would be overromanticizing it because mystics get lost and confused too."

Lukoff and others adopt William James's biblical reference point in distinguishing between the two states—"By their fruits you shall know them"—meaning that if a person is able to lead an ordinary life, one might consider his experience mystical, while another, who is lost in the chaos, could be labeled mentally ill. But Stern is unusual for a psychiatrist in the extent to which he resists the temptation to categorize and encourages you to resist it too. "Putting a definitive psychiatric diagnosis on somebody can be like judging somebody as evil. You're expressing your resistance to that person. As far as I'm concerned, to use words like 'health' and 'illness' is to make a judgment call that is not ultimately ours to make. We make it provisionally, but let's recognize that it's provisional."

"Let's go gently" is Stern's overall message to his colleagues. Let's not reduce things to all or nothing. Let's try to hold two, or three, or more ways of looking at health and illness at the same time. "I have patients who, perhaps because of their brain chemistry, confuse metaphor with outward reality. They see angels, or demons, and think those things are part of the outer world. But then again, there are people in this profession who have no sensitivity to metaphor, who think the world is literally only matter, that we are nothing but neurons. I consider that view as mistaken as the first. This is where pride comes in. A lot of our problems come down to the fact that we're all such know-it-alls that we're closed to other people's views and styles."

Stern was raised in a "very assimilated Jewish home," so assimilated that the family celebrated Christmas and even sang Christmas carols. Beyond that there was little religion in his upbringing, but both he and his twin brother were drawn to spirituality from an early age. "For some reason, at the age of twelve we asked our mother to get us *The Autobiography of a Yogi*. By the time I was in med school I'd already studied prayer and meditation for eight years." He describes his spiritual practice as "Zen meditation and devotional prayer, which are enriched by a sense of dialogue that comes from Buber and from being a psychiatrist."

While he believes there may be no essential difference between psychosis and mysticism, and that the whole business of diagnosing patients is open to question, in practice Stern isn't as out-on-a-limb as that sounds. He *does* diagnose patients, but he does it for mundane reasons—because the insurance company and the hospital want it, or as a shorthand for beginning discussion of a case with colleagues—and tries not to be seduced into seeing the patient as a mere manifestation of a particular illness, as an *It*. He works to open up the I-Thou landscape, to "confirm the other in his or her uniqueness." Then he may take things one step further. Where a patient has raised spiritual issues, he may bring up the idea of prayer or meditation.

Prayer plays a big part in Stern's life and work. He has edited a collection of Mother Teresa's thoughts on prayer and feels no compunction, after barely knowing an interviewer for an hour, asking, "Do you pray?" Prayer, he believes, has certain advantages over both psychotherapy and meditation, mainly because of its accessibility: "It's a language many people know well." Prayer, by its nature, involves a relationship with something that is outside oneself—at least as we ordinarily imagine the self—and larger than oneself. Whether literally or not, prayer puts you on your knees, puts you in a position of dependence, a place where individual limitations are acknowledged. Precisely who or what this larger, more powerful Other is, as far as Stern is concerned, is another matter, a theological issue. "Prayer gets you to the place where you realize we don't have very much control over things. Psychotherapy and meditation can get you there, too, in a more roundabout way. You could say that when psychotherapy gets you to that awareness, it is a form of prayer."

Stern doesn't suggest a prayer life if religion hasn't come up in the therapy—he makes it clear that he is not the patient's spiritual teacher, that he tries not to impose his own beliefs or agendas—but he also does not shy away from it. "I might ask, 'Do you believe in God?' If the answer is yes, I might ask, 'Do you pray?' Then I might suggest certain prayers from the person's faith tradition." He often recommends the psalms, because they are part of both Christian and Jewish heritage and because they are short prayers that "come from a very human place, often a place of distress."

In therapy, Neil Wolf told Stern of the joy he experienced in psychosis, and also of the spiritual emptiness he felt when he was normal. Staying on the medication, keeping the psychosis at bay, kept him shut off from the bliss that his illness brought, which he had come to cherish. He talked about wanting to develop a spiritual life of a more ordinary type. Stern responded by prescribing prayer, three times a day. Neil has diligently followed his doctor's orders, and it has helped him to stay on his medication. "I pray in the morning, at noon, and in the evening. I pray to Saint Dymphna, the patron saint of the mentally ill. The Franciscan Friars in Mount Vernon have a devotion to Saint Dymphna, and they print brochures with special prayers to her. I know them all by heart. It steadies me."

·   ·   ·

The case of Neil Wolf shows that a psychospiritual perspective on the part of a therapist does not come into play only with the extreme experience of psychosis but on a humbler plane as well. Neil's case might be said to involve two kinds of spirituality: the unmanageable high of psychosis and the low, grounded spirituality of prayer. Where David Lukoff helped Joshua Beil to see his psychosis in religious terms, in this case a psychiatrist is helping his patient *not* to reach for the spiritual high he got from his illness, but instead to find it, in less intense form, in the rest of his life.

That said, Stern also believes that so far Neil has only been partially successful in managing his illness. "Prayer has its own pitfalls. If being a psychotherapist and psychiatrist for so many years has taught me anything it is how we as humans have a great ingenuity for hiding. We hide from ourselves and from the real presence of the Divine. Prayer can be a hiding place."

While prayer has helped Neil, it has also, in Stern's view, kept him from living fully. Stern diagnoses Neil's maintenance of his illness in rather unusual terms: as a fear of adventure. Two subsequent trips that Neil made to Spain triggered psychotic episodes, and on a trip to Germany he decided that he was the reincarnation of Hitler and Christ. He went to an American military police station, told the officers that Armageddon was about to take place and that he wanted the missiles pointed toward Russia. The M.P. told him to go home; Neil bludgeoned him, and wound up in a military hospital in Heidelberg. Stern relates the physical act of journeying to Neil's psychotic adventures: "Many of us are either afraid of adventure or ride it too high. It's rare for most of us to be in a good middle zone, embracing adventure while still sober. We either ground ourselves too much and avoid the excitement and terror of living, or we get lost in the adventure. I think that relates very closely to the language and content of the spiritual traditions."

Adventure involves letting go of the familiar, which is what both the psychotic and the mystic do: release the self, let it fly up and join with something else, become a new self. Some of these flyers have faith: they trust that there will be a place to land. Others—lacking faith or maturity or strength or a support structure—go mad. "When Neil gets himself into a true adventure, he can't handle it. Then he becomes afraid of what happened, so he spends the rest of his life avoiding it, basically sitting at home." Neil doesn't disagree: "I spend most of my day watching the stock market—I have some stocks that I bought. I have friends who I visit once in a while. I see Dr. Stern. And that's it. I'm leading a dormant life."

Don Quixote has retired from the field, but nobody can fault him for that: nobody who has not experienced what he has can know what sort of pain he has lived through. The difference between the God of psychosis and the God of ordinary consciousness, perhaps, is how much of His face He allows one to see, and whether one can stand to see more than a tiny portion of it. "It's like the story of the Hasidic rebbe," Stern said. "Someone asks him, 'Rebbe, why do we pray for God's *tender*

6

At the Center for
the Spiritually Disturbed

God, to me, it seems, is a verb, not a noun.

—R. Buckminster Fuller

In 1270, King Louis IX of France died of the plague while en route to the Holy Land. As his body was carted back home in state, kneeling peasants lined the roads—all the way up the hot Italian peninsula, across the Alps, through the riverine valleys of southern France—to honor him as a saint. In the mind of the medieval peasant Louis embraced two worlds: the human (he sired eleven children and was a fierce warrior) and the divine (he was subject to religious visions and ruled with a remarkable benevolence). Eventually, the Catholic Church agreed with the people. In 1297, Louis was canonized as a saint.

When French fur trappers set up a trading post at the confluence of the Mississippi, Illinois, and Missouri rivers in 1764, they chose Louis as namesake. In doing so they symbolically planted the city of St. Louis, Missouri, in two realms, the everyday and the eternal. The symbolism carries over into contemporary reality: the home of Ralston Purina and Anheuser-Busch

St. Louis is also one of the most religion-soaked cities in the nation, a center of Jesuit learning, a birthplace of gospel music, a repository of Vatican Library treasures, the home of thousands of priests, nuns, and monks.

All of which may explain why St. Louis has become a focal point for spiritually centered psychiatrists and psychotherapists. George Grossberg, chairman of the Department of Psychiatry and Human Behavior at St. Louis University School of Medicine, said that his university is the largest Jesuit institution in the country, and that his department is a major Catholic Church referral center, to which priests, nuns, and bishops with mental health disorders come from all over the country.

The religiously oriented work is not confined to Catholics. Over time the word spread that here was a group of therapists who could deal with talk about God and sin as well as guilt and anger, and people of other religious backgrounds began showing up. Grossberg himself did his undergraduate work at Yeshiva University in New York. "I was a year away from becoming an orthodox rabbi when I switched gears and went to medical school. I was attracted to a Jesuit institution because I'm Jewish and believe in religion as an important force. And the people here said, 'We believe in and practice the Judeo-Christian ethic.'"

Psychologist Paul Duckro has been a professor at the university and a director of the St. Louis Behavioral Medicine Institute, which is affiliated with the university, since 1982. In 1991, Duckro started a new entity within the Institute called the Program for Psychology and Religion. It was originally supposed to be a place where religious professionals could come for psychotherapy, but a few years ago Duckro realized that more and more ordinary people from the community were coming to the program for treatment, attracted by the name. It occurred to him that clinical work that was sensitive to religion could be just as important to them as to priests and nuns, so he let the word go forth, through churches and some advertisements, that the program was open for business and taking all comers.

The Program for Psychology and Religion has become a success and is one of the few secular psychiatric programs in the country staffed by traditionally trained clinicians but devoted to joining its clients' psychological and spiritual selves. It is, in other words, a psychiatric center for the spiritually disturbed. Duckro put together an interdisciplinary team of psychiatrists, theologians, spiritual directors, priests, counselors, addiction specialists, a physical therapist, and an art therapist. The idea was that a psychotherapist could refer a patient to another team member as specific issues came up. Duckro makes clear that the Institute as a whole deals with the standard range of medical disorders—chronic headache, depression, self-injury behavior—and religious issues aren't foisted on patients. But, he adds, "We assume that spiritual issues are present in any problem," and thus the therapist will be as ready to go in that direction as, say, into childhood memories. "If someone has a problem with overeating, for example, and feels shame and guilt associated with it, you wonder to what extent that relates to 'I am no good, I have sinned.' Or with someone who becomes compulsive because they reject their sexual self, that could be part of a misreading of the teachings of their faith, a feeling that sex is evil."

Duckro has become part of the psyche-spirit network organized by David Larson and his National Institute for Healthcare Research: Larson has given his God-is-good-for-your-health talk here, and the St. Louis University School of Medicine is one of those that have received Templeton Foundation grants to give medical students training in religion. One component of the program requires students to follow chaplains on their hospital rounds, which students and instructors say has profoundly altered the students' idea of their profession. "The students' sense of a hospital completely shifts," one instructor said. "They see how much goes on when the physician isn't there. They see that the chaplain is an important part of a team, how much linkage the chaplains have between the nurses, the doctors, and the family. They see that the chaplain does a lot of translating, saying to the hospital staff, 'This is what's happening in the family, this is what they don't understand.' They are there when the chaplain prays with the patients. Some take part in the prayers. Others say they feel like they don't belong, or they feel inadequate."

Duckro himself is a devout Catholic who will go so far into the terrain of the spirit as to pray with a patient if he thinks it appropriate. This issue seems to define a fault line within the psyche-spirit movement. Most practitioners who believe that talking about God, sin, and redemption has a place in the therapy seem to draw the line at prayer. Tony Stern may suggest prayer as a part of treatment, but he believes that actually praying with a patient is not part of his job. Pfister Award–winner Paul Fleischman is overtly critical of the practice. With publicity given to studies that show health benefits of prayer, and polls reporting that significant numbers of people would like their doctor to pray with them in some situations, it is easy, Fleischman says, for the profession to slip across the line of what is acceptable. "To me, prayer is an inappropriate thing for a doctor to do," he said. "Psychiatry has swung from a bias against religion to a sanctimonious support for a new trend."

Duckro agrees that this is a danger, and says prayer in therapy is only appropriate in an overtly religious context, such as when the patient is a religious professional and/or has come into therapy with questions about religious observation and devotion. But he believes that far more harm has been done by therapists ignoring spirituality than by overemphasizing it.

"This idea of praying with clients is a very strange one for psychologists," he said. "I think it's part of an exclusivist secular attitude that has been dominant. But many people say they want a therapist who is sensitive to their faith. For years psychologists were cultivating a type of secular humanism that was, I think, unwittingly a violation. So I don't mind referring the patient back to their pastor, or encouraging the patient to pray."

Duckro instructs his staff to have patients do a "spiritual history" as they begin therapy, which consists of a simple list of questions about religious affiliation and beliefs. "This makes the patient aware of these issues as part of therapy, and it gives us a better idea of where the person is coming from." Of course, some people bristle at the very mention of religion. "Some people have such bad feelings about religion that they'll threaten to sue you if you bring it up. But then, the same is true about psychology."

As excited as he is about the expanding work with the general population, Duckro believes the program's work with religious professionals is particularly important. An intensive six-month program for priests and nuns in need of serious attention involves group therapy, cognitive therapy, and spiritual direction, as well as groups that discuss celibacy and dreams. The major problems that cause a diocese to send someone to the program include substance abuse and sexual misconduct. Thanks to the close relationship that Duckro has forged with the Catholic Church, this is a place where priests who have sexually abused altar boys may wind up.

The specialized religious clientele has given Duckro and his colleagues an opportunity to engage in some groundbreaking research. Duckro led a first-ever national study of sexual abuse among Catholic nuns, the results of which were published in 1998, and discovered that while the prevalence of sexual abuse is not much greater among nuns than it is among women in the general population (39.9 percent of nuns have experienced some form of sexual trauma in their lives, as compared to 25 to 30 percent of women as a whole), its effects can be particularly devastating among women in religious orders. Most exploiters, the study found, were members of the clergy, and "the most common role occupied by the exploiters was spiritual director."[1] In other words, the man that these woman came to for guidance of the most personal and vital sort violated his sacred trust in the most profound way possible. The result, according to the study, is typically "anger, shame, embarrassment, anxiety, confusion, depression, difficulty praying, and imagining God as 'Father' " and "thoughts of leaving religious life." Duckro hopes that this sort of research will help lead to the full integration of the psychological and religious lives of people in religious professions.

Duckro grew up in Dayton, Ohio, and went to a seminary school beginning at age thirteen. He always had the idea that one day he would be a priest, but became depressed in college and took that as a signal that he should leave the seminary. He shifted gears and got an M.B.A. which made him even more depressed, so he grew a beard and long hair ("this was my anti-war phase") and went into counseling. He was attracted to behavioral medicine. "My goal was to get away from this dualism: 'Is it psychological or is it medical?' " Now at age fifty he heads a program of which the entire purpose is to transcend that dualism, in part by bringing in the religion factor. "This has become a very hot topic in our field, but there is still a lot of resistance. Historically, science has opposed itself to faith, and that takes time to reverse. They were seen as alternative worldviews, but I don't think there is anything incompatible. Science is a way of knowing, but not a worldview that supplies meaning beyond what it can address. And religion must remember that it is not science—that's the mistake that creationists make."

• `·` •

Father Jim Byrnes is a middle-aged Catholic priest who in the midst of a deep depression worked with a traditional psychotherapist for a time without success. "Then I heard about the Program for Psychology and Religion, and knowing St. Louis University's reputation I thought it was worth a try." Paul Duckro became his therapist, and he immediately felt a difference. "Religion is so much a part of my life, and it made all the difference to have somebody who understands, who knows about faith. A lot of people wouldn't say to a priest, 'How's your prayer life?' They think, 'He's the one who knows about that sort of thing.' Paul was able to address the spiritual dimension."

As it turned out, there were spiritual and religious components to Byrnes's depression as well as a psychological one. "I'm gay, and I had divorced myself from my sexuality. I did this way back. One of the reasons I chose this profession, I know now, was to avoid dealing with my sexuality, which I couldn't face. I basically said, I don't have to deal with these things because I'm a priest."

His depression had gotten so severe that Byrnes was contemplating suicide, and since his brother had committed suicide, Duckro took the possibility seriously. "The spiritual side of the depression was that although I never stopped believing that God loved me, I stopped loving myself," Byrnes said. "Paul helped me to see that that was an affront to God; it was not valuing this life He gave me. That was a real spiritual awakening for me. Then there was the religious side of it, which is how do I, as a gay person, live in a church that is homophobic? Part of the genius of the way Paul worked was in getting me to see it all—the psychological, the spiritual, and the religious—as one big package."

Duckro suggested that Byrnes work with a spiritual director, a fellow priest who could take him further into church-related issues. He also prescribed a course in the spiritual exercises of

St. Ignatius of Loyola—a series of intense meditations meant to exercise and strengthen the soul the way a physical workout strengthens the body—which the spiritual director helped him to carry out.

The result of the therapy, Byrnes said, was spectacular. "Partly the depression had to do with my age. I'm forty-four, and have been on this path since my teens. In youth, there's a zeal, you're going to right all the world's wrongs. Then you get into your forties and you've accomplished some things—I've been director of a diocesan ministry and been pastor to different churches and a variety of ethnic groups—and you realize this is it, that you're in it for the long haul. So you start thinking, Is this what I want to do with the rest of my life? You start thinking maybe you would want to be with somebody in a love relationship.

"I now know that I'm a sexual being and have sexual desires. It's possible that someday I'll meet somebody and want to leave the priesthood. On the other hand, I'm happy where I am. A big part of it is acknowledging my sexuality as opposed to believing that sexuality equals genitality. I thought before that I didn't have to think about whether I'm gay or straight because I was celibate. Now what I say is I have sexual desires and there are people I'm attracted to, and just by saying that—I call it naming the thing—it doesn't have the power over you. So there are people I can talk to. I'll say, 'I'm so horny.' Or I'll say, 'I could just fuck his eyeballs out.' And those people know me and know I need to say those kinds of things. It's made me more comfortable in my own skin. Just because you have desires doesn't mean you have to act on them."

• • •

Tomás Agosin's influence extends to St. Louis. Paul Duckro's second-in-command at the St. Louis Behavioral Medicine

Institute is Fredrica Halligan, who studied under and was deeply influenced by Agosin, and then, after his death, replaced him on the Agosin Group panel at the Cape Cod Institute. While doing her graduate work at Fordham University, a Jesuit institution, and with Agosin as her model, Halligan found a way to link spiritual and clinical concerns. "It became part of my style," she said. "I also do a lot of dreamwork from a Jungian perspective, and that makes for a natural bridge." This was in the 1980s, when religion was still taboo in most psychological circles, but working at a Catholic university made it easier for her to, as she says, "come out of the closet spiritually. If I'd been working at a secular institution, or if I had had a supervisor who was telling me, as so many do, that that religion stuff is crazy, then it would have been very hard."

Halligan borrows more freely from various religious traditions than does Duckro. "I might recommend Buddhist meditations to Catholic clergy. What the Buddhists call mindfulness is similar to what the medieval church called recollection. Once in a while a conservative person will be uncomfortable being asked to take part in something from another tradition. But often what they're uncomfortable with is mysticism, which the church has always been wary of because it's an individual thing and the church has no control over it. The church prefers things that come through the sacraments."

Oddly, one of Halligan's most difficult challenges has been to put her religious patients in touch with their spiritual selves. "With the so-called humanizing changes of Vatican II, the Catholic Church lost some of the mystery of the faith. The devotion to the saints, the devotion to Mary—these were paths that would help people in their spiritual journey. But they kind of lost some of their energy and became seen as dull or inappropriate. Now with the influx of mystical traditions from the East, I think the Christian response is to tap into some of Christianity's contemplative and mystical roots."

One of her preferred ways of delving into the mystical and also grappling with some basic emotional issues of a celibate population is to examine the connection between sexuality and spirituality. "The medieval mystics were doing this centuries before Jung. Bernard of Clairvaux wrote forty-eight lectures on libido. He was trying to help his monks cope with celibacy by seeing the possibilities of a love affair with God, aiming for mystical energy rather than sexual energy." Such talk leads the priests and nuns into sharing their own spiritual moments. "One talked about going up in an air balloon, the feeling of closeness to God and the feeling of total freedom. You see the light in their faces as they share these stories. People don't realize it, but these people tend not to talk about what you might call spiritual experiences. They don't do it in seminaries or in religious orders. So when given a chance to describe their experiences they find it delightful."

Halligan also sees Protestant ministers as well as ordinary people from a variety of religious backgrounds. She believes that what is important is not that the religious tradition of the patient and therapist match but that the therapist has an active spiritual life. "If you're doing that kind of work yourself it doesn't matter what your orientation is because you'll be open to dealing with these issues. A Catholic can see a Protestant or a Jew. It's like cross-cultural counseling."

Like David Lukoff, Halligan believes that psychosis often has a genuine spiritual component. But, she says, "It's important to have your clinical antennae out so you recognize where something might be masquerading as spirituality. I had a self-mutilating patient who had a strong identity with Christ. Was she psychotic or in a genuine spiritual state? In this case, I concluded it was both. There was a mystical experience of the passion of Christ that was very genuine. That was different from her far more common pathology of cutting and burning herself." The therapy, then, revolved around getting the woman to separate her healthy spirituality from her self-destructive illness.

. . .

Stacy Davids is one of the more remarkable practitioners who have worked with Duckro and Halligan at the St. Louis Behavioral Medicine Institute. She is a biblical scholar as well as a psychiatrist, and her two specialties have influenced each other. As a New Testament scholar, Davids is a fellow of the Jesus Seminar, a feisty collection of biblical authorities who have applied the tools of history, archaeology, and various other professions to the search for the Jesus of history, and concluded that most of what is recorded in the gospels is not historically accurate. One of Davids's scholarly interests is in understanding how Jesus performed the so-called healing miracles. (New Testament scholars distinguish between the nature miracles— walking on water, turning water into wine, and so on—which most think probably did not literally happen, and the healings and exorcisms, about which opinions are divided but which many scholars think could be historically true.) Cultural psychiatry, Davids said, has edged the medical profession away from the mechanistic view of healing, according to which the body is a machine that the doctor fixes with certain drugs and tools. Studying the healing techniques of other cultures has led these psychiatrists to appreciate the role the mind plays in health and sickness. Davids believes that mind-body medicine can help provide an understanding of the faith healing that Jesus does in the gospels. By extension, she and others believe this interdisciplinary study can also help psychiatrists to excavate the various subterranean passages by which external events can translate themselves into mental or physical illness.

The Gospel of Mark, for example, tells the story (which is repeated in Matthew and Luke) of Jesus meeting a demon-possessed man in the town of Gerasa:

> And when he had stepped out of the boat, immediately a man out of the tombs with an unclean spirit met him. . . . Night and day among the tombs and on the mountains he was always howling and bruising himself with stones. When he saw Jesus from a distance, he ran and bowed down before him; and he shouted at the top of his voice, "What have you to do with me, Jesus, Son of the Most High God? I adjure you by God, do not torment me."[2]

Jesus exorcises the evil spirit, saying, "Come out of the man, you unclean spirit!" and then asks its name. "My name is Legion," the man replies, "for we are many." The demon then multiplies and enters the bodies of a herd of pigs, which, thus maddened, leap off a cliff into the sea. Christians have long puzzled over this curiously named demon. Blending cultural psychiatry with biblical scholarship yields interesting results.

The DSM-IV lists one cause of dissociative identity disorder (DID, formerly multiple personality disorder) as severe physical abuse during childhood. Jesus Seminar scholar John Dominic Crossan has pointed out that in an occupied territory the Latin word "legio" would have connoted a Roman army legion, and notes that similar-sounding folk disorders from various cultures involve possession by a spirit from the occupying power.[3] So in this reading Jesus' miraculous healing also had psychological and political aspects: the man's spirit possession could be read in psychiatric terms as originating from abuse at the hands of the Romans.* By extension, a psychiatrist faced with a case of DID might take into account social and even political forms of oppression, and might be open to the possibility, depending on the person's religious background, of "miraculous" healing.

Davids came to her current beliefs about psychiatry and religion in a very striking way. She is of Native American ancestry, and among her tribe, the Mohicans, Christianity is very important. During her childhood the family went to church twice a week; both of her parents are now ordained ministers.

After finishing medical school Davids did a residency in pathology and began working in a hospital. She developed a persistent cough during this time; a trip to the doctor revealed that she had a tumor in her lung and that she was suffering from Hodgkin's disease. "That was the most disturbing thing that's ever happened to me. One minute I was on track with my life and my career, and the next minute I had cancer." Thirteen months of intensive treatment eliminated the disease but left her devastated. "I got no support from people. My husband was contemplating whether we should get a divorce and he never visited me in the hospital, and I was far from my parents. I would lie in the dark in the hospital room feeling so totally alone and wondering whether anybody was out there."

She recovered, and went back to work after the ordeal, but there were problems. "My job was to sit in front of a microscope and diagnose disease. I might diagnose cancer a dozen times a day. In the past, I had been able to distance myself from it, to just see these as names on a piece of paper, but now they were

---

*The story also contains a dig at the Roman occupiers, whom the gospel writer identifies not only with unclean spirits but with pigs. As Crossan says, a demon "is consigned to swine; and is cast into the sea. A brief performancial summary, in other words, of every Jewish revolutionary's dream!"

real people to me. I knew what I was condemning them to." She became preoccupied with the people she had diagnosed, almost as if she had been responsible for their cancer. She took to looking up the people she had diagnosed with Hodgkin's disease and trying to help them. "I told them about cancer support groups I had found, which no one had helped me to find. I wanted to do something for them. But at the same time I felt weird because it wasn't my place to be doing this."

Soon she realized that she couldn't continue in her line of work. "I felt that I had gotten a second chance at life, and that this wasn't the life I wanted to have." She got a divorce from her husband, and applied for a residency in psychiatry at St. Louis University Hospital. But she had another concern, which was also left over from her illness. She had been raised in an intensely religious environment, yet she felt that her religion had failed her during the illness, when she needed it most. "I know that most people find their faith is reinforced during a crisis, but with me it was just the opposite. I felt this total loss of faith after my cancer experience."

The way she chose to deal with this problem was certainly out of the ordinary. She located all the seminaries in the St. Louis area and explored their programs. Finally she settled on one, Eden Theological Seminary, and enrolled in a graduate program in New Testament studies. For three years she did her psychiatry residency and seminary training simultaneously. Davids speaks in a soft, apologetic voice, which can be easily mistaken for meekness. Her wide, frank, almost unsettling gaze tells you that she has remarkable depths of resolve. "I think I'm really resourceful," she said when asked how she had come to this solution to her spiritual dilemma. "I work things until I find what fits me. I knew my religious faith was inadequate to withstand the cancer experience, so I had to explore it. I tend to be intellectual, so it was natural for me to explore Christianity in a scholarly way."

While at the seminary she became a fellow of the Jesus Seminar. The seminar's intently scientific approach to the texts of Christianity had an effect: "My traditional religious beliefs were debunked." At the same time, moving back and forth between seeing psychiatry patients and studying the gospels gave her an appreciation for the intricacies of the mind, how it can convert emotional trauma into physical illness. It dawned on her that in some ways what a psychiatrist does with a patient might be likened to what Jesus did to the demon-possessed man at Gerasa—maybe both kinds of healing involved unlocking secret doors of the mind. But she resisted the temptation to reduce faith healing to psychology. She preferred to consider that if there was a psychological element to the healing that Jesus did, there might also be a spiritual element to a psychiatrist's work.

At the end of Davids's quixotic path, she emerged as a psychiatrist with an unusually high sensitivity to religious and spiritual issues. She worked under George Grossberg at the University of St. Louis Hospital, where she became interested in ways to use the new DSM category to broaden her options in treating the patients she was seeing, some of whom were religious professionals. She met David Larson and became one of the first psychiatrists to teach the new religiously aware medical school curriculum that his National Institute of Healthcare Research had developed. Then she joined Paul Duckro's Program for Psychology and Religion and continued to refine her interest in the psyche-spirit connection before leaving for another St. Louis practice.

"Here's what I'm interested in," she said. "Let's say someone realizes that he doesn't believe in God, and he feels depressed about this. If he goes to an analyst, the analyst is going to say that his problem with atheism stems from his relationship with his authoritarian parents. What I'm interested in is, What if there is a God? What happens to that analyst's whole work? He didn't even begin to help that guy."

In place of that outmoded model she gives her ideal. "I want to do psychiatry that recognizes that there may be some God or power that helps us grow and change, and that is not external to the human being but is intrinsic to the human body. I believe our bodies contain mechanisms to heal, physically and psychically. I want to understand what those are."

Davids has seen her share of patients with psychospiritual ailments. "Some people come to a psychiatrist feeling guilty, which may relate to their beliefs. There are also people in real turmoil about their religious denominations, people who are in a crisis about whether their denomination really has 'the truth.' Many people develop a major depressive episode related to this kind of thing. And there are people who are using religion as a coping mechanism. You want to stay mindful of the psychological uses people put religion to serving."

One woman had an anorexic eating disorder that was directly related to her conservative Christian upbringing. Her church preached that sex was sinful; she would starve herself to the point where she stopped menstruating. It slowly emerged in therapy that she had rather strong sexual urges, which her unconscious battled by adopting an unusually strident asceticism. Davids concluded that the woman's spirituality was unhealthy because it restricted her from having a normal life. A goal of the therapy was to develop a more healthy religious life for the woman. Davids accomplished this by adopting a strategy that would be heresy in traditional psychiatry. "We read the Bible together. The woman used the Bible in her everyday life, and took it quite literally, but she only looked at certain parts, so we looked at other parts. We read the parts that showed Jesus going out and eating and drinking—he wasn't someone to restrict his caloric intake. We read some of the sensual passages. The idea was to open up her spirituality, and in that way give her a healthier psychological basis."

·   ·   ·

Another patient, a twenty-one-year-old named Pam Williams, came to Davids in a wheelchair and with an intricate blend of symptoms. Although her real name was Pamela, she insisted on being called Samson or Sam, and had in fact thought of herself as male since at least age ten. Her identity was not only male but super-male: she was nearly six feet tall and weighed two hundred and ten pounds, with blunt features and closely shaved hair. She tended to dress all in black and wear black wraparound sunglasses. Her speech was rough and occasionally threatening. She successfully passed herself off as male in most situations.

In psychiatric terms Pam/Sam presented a clear-cut case of gender identity disorder, which the DSM-IV says is characterized by "the desire to be, or the insistence that one is, of the other sex." Girls with GID refuse to wear dresses, tend to adopt a male name, and "their fantasy heroes are most often powerful male figures, such as Batman or Superman."[4] In Pam's case, however, her gender identity was entangled with her deep, evangelical religious beliefs: Samson isn't just any "fantasy hero" or strong man; he's *the* strong man, the holy warrior par excellence, who slew a thousand men with the jawbone of an ass.

A common feature of GID cases is childhood sexual abuse; between the ages of three and six Pam was routinely raped by a brother twelve years her senior. This abuse, which she referred to as "the training," had the bizarre effect of binding her to her brother; she seems to have modeled her tough-guy image on him. Throughout her childhood she developed the image. "Kids would make fun of me," Pam said. "I'd be, like, you don't even know me, dude. Then I found out if you hit someone they'll get scared of you. It was mostly guys. I'd start beating the tar out of them. It would take six or seven guys to pull me off." With puberty, Samson appeared, along with an involved patchwork of explanations to cover the discrepancy between how she felt on the inside and what her body was doing. Her lack of a penis was "a birth defect." When she began getting periods it was "a medical condition—my mom would give me one of those things and I'd stick it in my jockey shorts."

She had belonged to a series of churches and took an active part in the church social life. Most of the time she presented herself to the congregation as Samson. When she came to Davids she was in a wheelchair due to a mysterious paralysis that had come on some months earlier, in the wake of her only adult sexual encounter.

Davids worked with Pam in part by crediting and reinforcing her deeply held Christian beliefs. In one sense she used these beliefs in a fairly traditional way—to accomplish the therapeutic goals of exploring the paralysis and making Pam more comfortable with her gender identity. Any competent therapist, in other words, might encourage a patient to attend church if it seemed to benefit her psychologically. But Davids went deeper than that; she centered the therapy around Pam's "God image." She relied on the groundbreaking work by psychoanalyst Ana-Maria Rizzuto, publicized in her 1979 book *Birth of the Living God*, in which Rizzuto countered Freud's notion that God is a manifestation of neurosis by studying how children from a variety of backgrounds and age groups understand and use the concept of God. Rizzuto found that the concept of God is like a living thing within a child, which grows and changes as the child grows, and which is closely tied to parental attitudes and other forces in the child's upbringing. Among other things, she found a close correlation between "God image" or "God representation" and self-image. "These studies show that self-image and God image go hand in hand," Davids said. "When Pam first came to me, she saw God as a god of revenge who sends people to hell. Your God image comes from various pieces of your life. Influences on her God image were her father, who abandoned the family when she was a child, her brother, who abused her, and an evangelical Christian background."

People who have such a severe concept of God, Davids said, tend to have low self-esteem, and in Pam's case Davids began to suspect that the paralysis had to do with her self-esteem and her relationship with her mother as well as the sexual experience. "Freud said behavior is multiply determined. Pam is a good example of that. There are so many layers to each symptom." On one level was her conflicted, almost tortured, attitude toward sex. Although she always found sex "totally disgusting," she also admitted that she would feel sexual urges but be unable to act on them. Due to the abuse she had endured as a child she found the physical act of sex so abhorrent that, in the one instance when she tried it, the lower half of her body shut down in revolt.

On another level, Davids suspected, the paralysis related to self-esteem. Pam had turned twenty-one during this time, the age at which one is supposed to be responsible for oneself, and instead she was living with her mother with no end to the dependence in sight. "Her inability to walk was displaying her inner conflict, needing to walk away from her mother in conflict with the drive to be an infant and be cared for."

Davids diagnosed the paralysis as "a classic conversion disorder psychodynamic. It's like a soldier whose arm becomes paralyzed during war." The DSM-IV defines conversion disorder as one in which there is a loss of motor or sensory ability for which there is no medical basis. The *Synopsis of Psychiatry* gives the standard psychoanalytic cause as "repression of unconscious intrapsychic conflict and the conversion of anxiety into a physical symptom. The conflict is between an instinctual impulse (for example, aggressive or sexual) and the prohibitions against its expression."[5]

Some experts relate conversion disorders to dissociative disorders. In both, a portion of the personality breaks off or dissociates itself from the rest. In conversion disorder it is a bodily function—hearing, sight, limb control—while in dissociative identity disorder it is a portion of the individual's identity that splits off. Biblical scholar Stevan Davies, whose book *Jesus the Healer: Possession, Trance and the Origins of Christianity* brings cultural psychiatry to bear on New Testament scholarship, believes that Jesus' healings all fall into one or the other of these categories, and even draws up a "dissociative scale for peasant Galilee"—a list of those persons Jesus healed, ranging from less to more profoundly dissociative cases. Davies rates a case of blindness that Jesus cures (Mark 8:22) as a comparatively mild conversion disorder, while total demonic possession is at the severe end, a pure dissociative identity disorder.[6] In all of these cases, the ailment was seen in the culture as related to sin; healing was achieved by cleansing the soul. "If we assume the psychological theory that sin is guilt or trauma projected out onto a god figure," writes Davies, "then the elimination of sin is, psychologically speaking, formal permission to forgive oneself."[7]

During the course of the therapy, Pam's God image softened. She spoke about "God's love," about wanting to be a conduit for it, to help others see that Jesus loved them. There were two major positive outcomes to the therapy. In terms of gender identity, Pam made a decision to go by her given name rather than Samson, and to allow people to refer to her as "she." The decision was Pam's: Davids didn't encourage her to "go female," only to reach a place of stability in her identity. Pam took up a form of karate, a move that Davids applauded:

"Karate is a way for her to be female but live these masculine qualities."

Also during the course of the therapy, Pam's paralysis, which had kept her in a wheelchair for a year, was "healed" as a result of a group prayer session that her church's congregation conducted on her behalf. Davids believes the change in Pam's God image opened her to the faith healing—as God became a loving God, Pam's self-esteem rose; she came to feel herself worthy of God's love. In biblical terms, she was cleansed of sin and healed.

What distinguished Davids's treatment of Pam was not her own religious convictions (Davids admits that she changes her mind from time to time on whether she herself believes in God) but her commitment to exploring the deep interrelationship of the patient's psychological and spiritual lives. "Most therapists probably wouldn't be comfortable working with a patient at the level of God image," she said, "because most are unfamiliar with the concept, and with the literature on it. I think they would feel unqualified to deal with the topic."

With such practitioners, the St. Louis Behavioral Medical Institute is a glimpse of a possible future, one in which bodily health flows naturally into spiritual health. If this is the future, it is also in some ways a step backward. Throughout the ancient world medicine was held to be a sacred art. Asclepius may represent the apotheosis of the kind of doctor Paul Duckro and Stacy Davids aspire to be: a physician of Homeric Greece who was so revered for his healing powers—for his understanding of the connections between body, psyche, and soul—that later generations revered him as a god. His connection with modern psychology is particularly arresting: later physicians had their patients sleep in temples devoted to him and would decide on a course of treatment only after hearing the patients recount their dreams.

Of course, the divine healer is not unique to Greece. According to biblical scholarship the history behind the New Testament reveals something very similar: a man with a profound insight into the full nature of human beings uses this insight to heal, to make the blind see and the lame walk, and this power that he seems to wield is so astonishing to those who witness it that he too is lifted out of the normal realm of life, to another plane of being:

> "I say to you, stand up, take your mat and go to your home." And he stood up, and immediately took the mat and went out before all of them; so that they were all amazed and glorified God, saying, "We have never seen anything like this!"[8]

7

The Patients of Job

For the arrows of the Almighty are in me;
my spirit drinks their poison;
the terrors of God are arrayed against me.

—JOB 6:4

A hot and windy June day in Cambridge, Massachusetts. Warm breezes come in through the open windows. Eight people shuffle into the room and take seats on random pieces of furniture: folding chairs, a weathered sofa, a piano bench. As they settle themselves, the languor that held them out in the institutional hallway vanishes; an eagerness, or perhaps edginess, creeps in. A woman in her thirties leans over and warns a visitor not to talk about astrology. "It's not allowed."

"That's not true," an older woman named Connie declares. "It's a belief—any kinds of beliefs are fair game."

The meeting has begun.

David, a Jewish man in his twenties, announces, "I don't believe in anything. I'm an atheist. Can you please explain the Holocaust to me? How could God have let the Holocaust happen?"

"I believe in God *and* evolution," says Connie, by way of response. "I think you can believe in both."

Someone else begins to speak, but is cut short by David. "I believe in Darwin, in hard determinism, not in free will. That's the only way to make sense of what Hitler did to the Jews." His face becomes flushed when he talks; his voice is loud but he sits back defensively in his seat.

A lively and rather profound discussion starts. Does evil exist? Is illness a sign of God's disfavor? Does God's love cover all people equally? Is hatred ever justified? But again David interrupts with his signature refrain: "Explain to me the torture of the German scientists, the things they did to the Jews. . . ."

He finishes his thought, there is a brief pause, and then the lean and elegantly attired middle-aged woman who is leading this discussion cocks her head and says, in measured, graceful cadence, "David, this just occurred to me. I wonder if you see your illness as a torture. I wonder if at some level you think that understanding how the Holocaust happened could help you to understand your illness."

A little flicker registers on David's face, he gives a long sigh, and then he nods rapidly and says, "Yes. Yes. Yes."

Whereupon an older woman with sad-gentle eyes gives voice to what has just happened: "That's an insight! A real insight! I never understood why you always talk about the Holocaust."

This is not, of course, an ordinary conversation about religion. All of these people have serious mental illnesses; many have spent large portions of their lives in institutions. They have had religion systematically denied them, thanks to an odd and unintended collusion between Freud and the Constitution: while the mental health profession has traditionally divorced itself from matters of the spirit, public mental health facilities have also shied from anything that smacks of religion for fear of "separation of church and state" complaints.

It is one thing to operate a clinic in which a functioning person can talk about God in psychotherapy or discuss a past psychotic episode in spiritual terms. Here, at the far frontier of the psyche-spirit movement, is an effort to bring issues of religion and spirituality to the very sickest of the mentally ill. These are the people whose lives have been ruled by mental institutions; they are generally the ones least able to stand up and speak for themselves. Psychologists are only now beginning to understand how devastating this whitewashing of religion has been for them. Ironically, these people may have a greater need than most to grapple with questions of ultimate meaning. According to traditional psychology, they are also the one group for whom religion poses an actual danger.

Research on how people with serious mental illness deal with religious and spiritual issues has largely been in the hands of one woman, the woman who led this discussion and who—thanks to the new interest in exploring religion as a factor in health, and in particular to the work of David Larson—is on the verge of carrying out a transformation in the way mental institutions view spirituality. Larson, who has worked with most of the major players in the psyche-spirit movement, doesn't mince words in talking about her: "Nancy Kehoe is one of the most important people in the country."

Nancy Kehoe was a Catholic nun first, then a psychologist. Coming to the profession from a wholly religious background gave her a certain perspective and also a boldness—she would say a naïveté—to bring about change. She entered a cloistered convent of the Religious of the Sacred Heart order in 1956, at age eighteen. She would probably have remained in the cloister and lived her life shut off from the outside world were it not for Pope John. The council of reforms that became known as

Vatican II included the decree that religious orders that involved themselves in the world—and the Sacred Heart order specialized in teaching—ought not to be shut off from it. Overnight, life changed. The eighteen-year-old girl who went inside emerged in 1968 a thirty-year-old woman. Along with the end of the cloistered life came other reforms: instead of assigning sisters randomly to teaching posts, the order instituted psychological testing to ascertain what their particular skills and aptitudes might be. Kehoe got high marks, especially in social service. She had received an undergraduate degree while cloistered; she now went on to do a master's in counseling, then a Ph.D. in counseling psychology at Boston College.

In 1975, she was assigned to do postdoctoral clinical work at Cambridge Hospital, and suddenly found herself in alien territory. Her colleagues, proper godless mental health professionals all, mistrusted her, challenged her, wondered how someone wedded to the mildewed ideology of religious belief could possibly have the clarity of mind and intellectual honesty to confront real psychological problems. Kehoe challenged them right back. "I had spent all these years in the religious life, and now I found myself in this setting where *nobody* mentioned religion at all," she said. "It was totally ignored and excluded from all talk of patients and their problems. I was fascinated. I mean, at a case conference about a twenty-one-year-old Irish-Catholic woman having an abortion, no one asked how her religious beliefs might enter in."

She started questioning her colleagues. Why *not* inquire into a patient's religious life and beliefs? Aren't such things as pertinent to a psychological profile as one's sexual life and beliefs?

Kehoe's line of inquiry might have been summarily dismissed, but a savior stepped forward. The head of psychiatry at Cambridge Hospital was John Mack, who would later become renowned as the Harvard psychiatrist who put his academic respectability on the line in championing the alien abduction phenomenon. Mack had just been to France, where he had become interested in mystics' claims to be able to hear voices and see visions. He was delighted to have a nun on the hospital's staff, someone who could speak both the language of psychology and of religion. They spent hours together discussing where the two languages might overlap.

The fact that so revered a psychiatrist took her seriously gave Kehoe credibility with her colleagues, and gave her the courage to explore her interest. She did a pilot study in which she surveyed two hundred clinicians in the Boston area and found that fewer than one in five asked suicidal patients about religious beliefs. "I mean, if someone is suicidal, wouldn't it be natural to ask, 'Where do you think you're going to go when you die?'" Kehoe said, still bewildered today at this massive blind spot in her second profession. (This is all the more impressive when you consider that 10 percent of people diagnosed with schizophrenia commit suicide.) She then examined the ten major "suicide scales"—standard lists of questions to put to a potentially suicidal patient—and found only a single question that mentioned religion, and that parenthetically.

Soon colleagues started to come to her with confessions: patients regularly brought up religious material in therapy—Is my illness a punishment from God? I know I suffer from delusions, but sometimes I also feel God's presence: how do I tell which is which?—and the psychologists had no idea how to handle it, so they tended to let the concerns and questions sputter. "Soon," Kehoe said, "it was, 'If a patient mentions God, call Nancy.'" This, she felt, was a positive step, but it didn't begin to tackle the overarching problem that the entire mental health system was ignoring a major feature of mental life.

Kehoe developed a religious assessment tool,* a list of questions to help clinicians and their patients talk about such issues: Were you raised in a religious tradition? As a young child, did you think about God/a Force/a Supreme Being? Can you describe how you imagined that Being? Some in the field wonder whether there is a subtle evangelizing taking place in such questionnaires, to which Kehoe has a set response: "Just because you ask a person if they believe in God does not mean that you do, or even that you think religion is good or bad. You're simply saying that this is an important area of people's psychic life, and that understanding it deepens your understanding of a person." The challenge she presented to her colleagues then, and continues to present today, stated in her own words, is this: "With clinicians who don't believe in God, can they believe that others *can* believe, or do they think religious belief is just a psychological phenomenon, a defense?" The difference is important, she thinks, because on the one hand a therapist will tend to want to help a client "get over" religion, while on the other the therapist will be inclined to give room, to be alert for places where religion may be used as a crutch or defense but not reduce it to being merely that.

But more important than challenging her colleagues, Kehoe wanted to do something for the chronically mentally ill, whose lives were ruled by the mental health profession, whose self-identities had been scrunched and punched and levered into DSM diagnoses, who were encouraged to think of themselves as suffering from an organic disease, with the supposedly liberating corollary that it was not their fault that they had been yanked out of the normal courses of life and were left to wander and struggle for a basic rational foothold. Some of

*Several other mental health professionals have created such tools. Probably the one that has been most influential was that developed by psychologist James Fowler. He and his colleagues administered his questionnaire to four hundred people over an eight-year period and used the results to paint a portrait, detailed in the 1981 book *Stages of Faith*, of how people develop faith and meaning in their lives.

them no doubt gained some comfort from that, but Kehoe knew from experience that the men and women locked in institutions or doing time in halfway houses while attending day treatment programs wrestled with questions of ultimate meaning not less but more than those leading more normal lives. Their illness keeps them trapped in a "liminal state," an in-between state. They stand outside society, watching others catch trains and plan vacations, order Chinese takeout for business lunches, hoard time to spend with their children, put money into IRAs, buy antiques, get the car fixed, caress their lovers, be late for meetings, settle conflicts, plant geraniums. Such unending bustle might seem absurd at times to those involved in it, but not to these people. To them, it is life itself: life that they are excluded from. It is a river, and they are left to stand on the banks watching all those who knew how to swim.

Standing there, they have both time to ponder and a great deal to ponder. *Why me?* They are natural philosophers, natural theologians. They are all Job, laid low by God, overwhelmed with reasons to despise God. For the rest of us, meaning-of-life questions are things to be pondered in off-moments, easily forgotten as we burrow down into our world of transactions. But for many of the people Nancy Kehoe knew and worked with, ultimate meaning wasn't a pastime or the subject that filled an hour on Sunday morning; it was a constant gnawing presence, a way of life, whether they wanted it to be or not.

How, Kehoe wondered, could the system not provide them with a forum to ease the hammering psychological burden that came with their illness? Forget religion: this was a matter of psychological agony, a life spent enduring both a crippling illness *and* the emotional assault that the illness brings on, the nagging or shrieking, insidious or pervasive voice that says: *This is my fault. Somehow, I brought this on myself. God is punishing me. I'm not just an inferior person—I'm an inferior soul.* If the system was keeping this kind of deep and abiding anguish locked inside these people, wasn't it actually abetting their mental illness?

In 1981, Kehoe proposed to start a spirituality discussion group at a Cambridge day treatment center, whose patients included people suffering from depression, schizophrenia, manic depression, and psychosis. The staff were hesitant: this seemed a basic violation. They were there to provide a haven of rationalism, to protect patients from flights of fancy, visions, delusions, unreal thinking. To bring the historically destabliz- ing element of religion into the clinical setting could defeat its whole reason for being.

Kehoe let the fear work itself out in debate. Staff members pointed to the standard psychological view regarding religion and serious mental illness, which held that religious talk would fan the flames of psychotic delusion. Other staffers feared that if offered the "escape" of religion, patients would retreat into it. Some foresaw anarchy, with patients and staff dividing along sectarian lines.

Kehoe extracted from these reactions what she called "some of the staff's own ambivalence about religion and spiri- tuality" and an assumption that the patients—whose IQs and level of education might very well match or exceed that of the staff—were somehow unable to engage in thoughtful meaning- of-life discussions. She pushed, and got the go-ahead for a trial discussion group.

That was in 1981. The "Spiritual Beliefs and Values" group at Fresh Pond Day Treatment Center in Cambridge is still run- ning. A few years later Kehoe started a similar program at another local day treatment center for the chronically mentally ill. It too is still running. From the beginning, the groups were psychotherapeutic rather than didactic: free-form discussions, not sermons-of-the-day. There were two ground rules: no prose- lytizing and respect differences.

In both places, staff members were astonished at the results. It was like turning on a tap—a flow of opinions, fears, and beliefs issued forth. Jews, Christians, Muslims, and atheists, aged twenty to over sixty, wondering aloud about who God is, discussing whether it's okay to feel angry at God, and querying fellow members from other religious backgrounds: "In your tradition, are there examples of God's anger or are there examples of people crying out in anger toward God?" They asked the questions we all ask, only with more urgency: What is evil? What is sin? Did I do something that God gave me this illness? Am I atoning for some sin my parents committed?

The groups have also spent considerable time trying to sort out the difference between religious experience and psychotic experience. Kehoe is sympathetic to talk of visions and voices; her own path in life began with what a traditional psychologist would call an auditory hallucination. She was a high school girl praying in an empty chapel when someone or something said to her, "I want you to go to Kenwood." Kenwood was the name of the novitiate of the religious order she eventually joined. Kehoe tried to put into words what that intensely personal and transcendent moment—a calling in the most literal sense—was like: "The most striking thing about it to me was that it felt as if it wasn't self-generated. I have compared it with other times when I was trying to convince myself to do something, for example, but this was different—there was no internal dynamic. It was a very specific time: it was January, and we were making a weekend retreat. I was praying in the chapel. It felt like hearing a voice, but not like someone called my name. But it felt like a clear, specific message, so it felt external but it felt internal." Regarding the groups, she said, "If someone tells us he saw Jesus, we listen. The comment isn't taken apart in a subtly pejorative way."

But that doesn't mean out-of-the-ordinary experiences are

not hashed over. Most spiritually attuned psychologists seem to agree that analyzing a potential religious experience, subjecting it to some reality testing, is healthy, and in that spirit Kehoe's groups have pored over their own experiences. Interestingly, some members have determined that a growing religious preoccupation is a signal of illness, that, for example, their bipolar disorder is moving into a manic phase, while others have said that the onset of a feeling of spiritual well-being is their clue that they are coming off a bad period, returning to wellness. They are providing evidence, in other words, that the connection between mental illness, mental health, and religion is complicated.

Almost at once, staff members were won over by the spirituality groups. They saw group members become livelier, less pent-up, transferring their newfound energy into other discussion groups. In more than eighteen years, Kehoe says, not a single patient participating in the groups has suffered an increase in delusions: a complete repudiation of accepted psychological wisdom.

Which is not to say that delusion is not a factor. Often a patient will come into a meeting in the throes of a delusional state, which Kehoe handles with aplomb: "Once, a man kept interrupting the group, saying that he was Jesus Christ and saying to me, 'I want you to tell me that I'm Jesus Christ!' I just said, 'Jacob, I'm not qualified to make that judgment.'" If a patient becomes too disruptive, he is asked to leave that session and come back after the episode has passed.

Indeed, the group meetings are far from placid. Sitting in on them, one catches flickers of anger, annoyance, intolerance, and conflict; in short, they are serious discussions of religion. Kehoe thinks anger is as important an outcome as loving kindness; it gives the patients a chance to see how their emotional and spiritual lives are intertwined.

Kehoe's most pointed example of how ignoring religious issues can result in therapy missing its mark occurred several years earlier. A woman in her late thirties was in a psychiatric treatment program; she had run away from home as a child and grew up in foster care. She spent years on the streets, had been a prostitute and a drug addict, and had attempted suicide several times, the earliest when she was eight. She had been in and out of the mental health system for years and had had a succession of psychotherapists. Kehoe was asked to talk to her because God had come up in recent conversation with a clinician.

Kehoe began by doing a religious profile of the woman. As they discussed the kind of church she had been taken to as a girl, the woman made a startling confession that she had been "born in sin," that she was the child of her mother and her mother's father. This, she told Kehoe, was the root of all her problems. She believed that she was fundamentally evil. "I've always thought of myself as spiritually ill," she said.

"Everyone was just amazed that in all her years of psychiatric treatment and substance abuse programs, this fact had never been revealed," Kehoe said. "So, if you don't ask these questions, you can fail to find out serious issues." Kehoe began working with the woman in earnest by suggesting that she was angry with God. The woman didn't understand the concept, and said such a thing wasn't possible. Kehoe believes this is common not just among the mentally ill but in society: people who don't allow their spirituality to develop and mature along with their intellect tend to have a childish view of God; they don't see that questioning, defying, arguing with, redefining, and renaming God is part of what it means to be a spiritual person. "I told her there is a long tradition of people being angry at God. I told her about Job. I used the psalms—'My God, why have you abandoned me?' She was impressed, and we took it from there."

The spirit of Job seems to hover over Kehoe's work. Many mentally ill people are ambushed by their illness in the midst of normal, full lives, mowed down by it, stripped of everything they valued, and left to wonder why. The book of Job describes a man who was both devout and enormously successful, an entrepreneur of the Bronze Age, until one day tragedy struck and he lost his home, his wife, his children, his cattle, his land. Staggered by fate, he did not so much abandon God as abandon himself, despise himself. Many of the people locked in institutions or stumbling around halfway houses, flipping through memories of a different, long-ago life echo his words in one way or another:

> Why did I not die at birth,
>   come forth from the womb and expire?
> Why were there knees to receive me,
>   or breasts for me to suck?
> Now I would be lying down and quiet;
>   I would be asleep; then I would be at rest.[1]

A woman named Andrea addressed a conference called Spirituality and Recovery from Mental Illness, at which Nancy Kehoe spoke. She was an African American in her forties, a large, cheerful, articulate woman, a graduate of Tufts University who works in a program helping people to recover from childhood trauma. She sat before fifty mental health professionals and told her story, her hands shaking uncontrollably but her voice clear and eerily serene: "Throughout my childhood I was constantly raped by my father and beaten by my mother. I became pregnant by my father, and had his child. I learned to live entirely in my head, where I was safe and omnipotent. There was only one huge glitch: I began cutting and burning myself. I have been in psychiatric institutions for thirty-two years."

Andrea developed dissociative identity disorder as a way to deal with the prison of her childhood. "My only partner to help me survive that suffering was my concept of God," she said later. "With God's help, I created alternative selves to have other people in it with me. If I needed to be angry, my predominant self couldn't show it, but I could turn into Sandra, who could be very angry and foulmouthed and vengeful. If sad and demure was called for, the Girl in the Old-fashioned Dress came out. When my father was attacking me, and I needed to lure him out of the violence, Sara would appear, and she was good at seductive behavior, she could lure him into lustful behavior as a way to protect me."

Religion remained vital for Andrea as she worked through the disorder—as with Job, giving up religion just wasn't an option for her. Also like Job, she did not simply repeat pieties but let her religion—her idea of God, her sense of fate, her understanding of the relationship between herself as an individual and the yawning chasm of the universe—rage and twist through her. She hasn't stayed true to Baptist theology for reasons that seem awfully sound. "How can I believe in the Virgin birth after incest?" Instead, she has become a searcher, and she says her spiritual search has been a part of her recovery. "I've constantly worked through my religious beliefs. Right now I'm struggling with the idea of whether or not I believe in Christ. I can't believe God would sacrifice a human being, especially his own son, for the good of anybody. I think this struggle has to do with my own history of child abuse. But I've learned that as adults we have to grow out of our childish ideas of religion. I've learned that you don't need an abstract language to talk about spirituality. You don't even need to say 'God.' You just recognize. Recognize your children, give them your time, tell them they are real and valuable. I was made to feel invisible as a girl, and that was devastating. Recognize others. That's where spirituality is."

Spirituality, as Job knew and as the questers in Nancy Kehoe's groups seem to feel, whatever its trappings and ideology, can be boiled down to some basics, and one of them is the search itself. It may involve cursing oneself, or giving God the finger. "The greatest thing a therapist ever told me," Andrea said, "was that anger is a gift from God."

Surprisingly, when asked what participating in Kehoe's spirituality groups meant to them, few people said that it had helped them to better understand their illness or that it had made them more religious. Some said they were more confused, but energized. One said, "It has challenged my faith. It has made me think about how I think about God. My idea of who God is is different now."

"It isn't always easy to look at what you believe," another group member said. "In this group, I learned that it was okay to be angry at God and at some of the things the church has done to me. I was pestered to death by my grandmother about religion, but here I learned that I have a spiritual quest that can be separated from religion."

What is interesting about these responses is that they seem no different from the way people without mental illness might react to a serious, ongoing discussion about religion. This, of course, is Nancy Kehoe's point. A religious life is something we all have, and with anyone, mentally ill or not, religious issues commingle with psychological ones. But, Kehoe says, we tend not to give the chronically mentally ill the dignity of having genuine religious beliefs. "If a Harvard professor says he had an out-of-body experience, or if he says he prays to his dead relatives, it is accepted," she told the conference on spirituality and recovery from mental illness. "If a mentally ill person says the same thing, we immediately assume it's part of the illness." And that is why she feels these groups are so important. Mentally ill people may hide or mask their religious sensibilities out of fear that other people will read them as an expression of their illness.

As the years went by, Kehoe's spirituality groups continued to be successful, but small. She maintained them as, in effect, community gardens, two small places where a few lives could be allowed to flourish in ways that had once been impossible. Otherwise she devoted herself to the private psychotherapy practice she had built up, worked as area director for her order ("sort of a middle management position"), and spoke at occasional seminars and workshops on the topic of spirituality and psychotherapy. Several years ago she met Peter Cohen, and since then she has been part of the Agosin Group at the Cape Cod Institute.

Then, sometime in the mid 1990s, something happened. Health care officials started showing up at her workshops. Her topic—bringing the religious worldview into the psychological worldview—was becoming hot. She got a call from a psychologist in Milwaukee named John Prestby, who had seen her give a talk called "How Psychology Lost Its Soul" and was interested in having her come to talk to his colleagues at a public mental health facility. She did, and the reaction was strikingly different from that of her colleagues twenty years earlier. "People on the staff here were very excited about what Nancy had to say," said Prestby, who is the clinical program director for the day treatment program at the Milwaukee County Mental Health Division. "She even went so far as to argue that if you neglect the religious side of a patient's life, it could be an ethical issue. People here were ready to hear that: it came at a great time."

The result was that the Milwaukee County Mental Health Division, a government organization, hired Kehoe to set up similar spirituality groups throughout their system, and to train their staff members to run them. The Milwaukee organization serves twenty thousand people a year and has an annual budget of $130 million; it operates two nursing homes, a hospital for children, and a hospital for adults. Mental health programs in several other states are interested in doing something similar.

Kathleen Eilers, the chief administrator of the Milwaukee County Mental Health Division and the woman who gave the go-ahead for Kehoe to bring religion into a public mental health setting, personifies the change in her field. She was trained as a psychiatric nurse, and she spent years working in the public mental health system. Then, in the mid-1990s, the issue of "how to create a spiritual life for people with mental illness" arose in conversations with several colleagues. "Psychiatry has prided itself on keeping its distance from religion," she said, "and there's always been a lot of talk about the religious preoccupation that is symptomatic of major mental illness, how one needs to stay away from that. But I came to feel that we had deprived people of an enormous aspect of their lives. So we had Nancy come here, and everything she said was right where we were. So we said that in a low-key way we would attempt to do something about it."

As far as Eilers knows, hers is the first government-run mental health system that is so boldly venturing into the territory of religion. "In a public institution, of course, there is the question of whether this is mixing church and state. But nobody said a word. We've been clear about the competency of the people running the groups, and clear that this isn't proselytizing or selling something, and it's all voluntary for the patients."

As of late 1998, the Milwaukee spirituality groups had been running for one year, in long-term care programs, an outpatient clinic, and day treatment programs, and Eilers is clear about the results. "It's the one thing here that I'm most proud of. It's too much to say that we've become a spiritual haven, but we've created a space where that is nurtured. Now we even have comments from staff about their own spiritual lives and needs.

They're wondering whether we need a spiritual discussion group for the staff." When a comment is made that this is possibly uncharted territory for a government mental health organization, Eilers doesn't flinch: "Are you kidding? It's radical!"

Kehoe has felt the wind change and has responded. In 1998 she gave up her private practice and began devoting herself full-time to setting up similar programs around the country. She has received encouragement from her peers because she has quelled some longstanding concerns about the relationship between religion and serious mental illness. But, as she herself would admit, she hasn't provided definitive answers.

Indeed, you could say that Kehoe has done little more than open the door into a whole new arena of psychospiritual exploration. Once we are inside, the hard work remains; questions that people have asked for centuries are still to be answered. Some of the most pressing, in a world where religious and nationalistic fervor can lead to mass horror, have to do with the relationship between religious violence and mental instability. Is it possible for religious passion to lead to mental illness? And not just to mental illness but to outright madness—the kind of madness that threatens not only the individual but society?

8

Crusaders

*What do the victims matter if the
gesture is beautiful?*

—Laurent Tailhade

He was twenty-two years old, a good Catholic who went to Mass every Sunday. He was the only son of a dental technician and a piano teacher; he had dropped out of college and was working in a beauty salon. The illness had started a year or so earlier, with hallucinations and an increasing religious preoccupation. By now his delusional system was fully established: the Catholic Church was being persecuted by a vast subterranean conspiracy led by the Freemasons and involving the world's major corporations. Catholics were being forced out of jobs and into the margins of society, and Masonic physicians were secretly injecting a substance into the scrotums of Catholic males that rendered them sterile.

The solution to this looming catastrophe was three-fold. Catholics had to avoid credit cards, which had a computer chip embedded in them that was "the mark of the beast" spoken of in the Book of Revelation. The Vatican had to begin counterfeiting U.S. dollars and commence a worldwide infusion of wealth to its flock. And Catholic women had to stop having abortions. This last point was vital, for their actions violated God's commandments and reduced the Catholic population, furthering the goals of the conspirators.

His name was John Salvi. As was the case with Joshua Beil and Neil Wolf, Salvi's illness, which would later be diagnosed as schizophrenia, had come on in early adulthood. As with theirs, it involved florid delusions. And like Neil Wolf, John Salvi acted on his delusion. He plugged himself into the militant fringe of the anti-abortion movement, consumed its literature on "justifiable homicide," bought a semiautomatic rifle and spent time at a firing range.

"This is what you get!" he shouted as he entered the first of two Boston-area abortion clinics in December 1995. "You should pray the rosary!"[1] Then he squeezed the trigger and sent a spray of hollow-point bullets into the room. When his spree was over, two women were dead and five other people injured.

• • •

Waco, Bosnia, the World Trade Center bombing, the blast at the federal building in Oklahoma City, Heaven's Gate, the Om Shinrikyo gas attacks in Japan, the bombing of American embassies in Kenya and Tanzania, the threat of nuclear war between India and Pakistan. It is possible to scan such a list of calamitous news items of the 1990s without realizing that they all have religion at their core. Most of these events were precipitated by someone or some group who believed, like John Salvi, that the transcendent Principle of Love demanded that bloodshed and/or terror rain down on humanity.

Religion-inspired violence presents a challenge to the psyche-spirit movement. The rationale behind the movement is that religion is a natural—that is, healthy—part of the human being, and that psychology's failure to recognize this has led to pain and suffering. But *is* it healthy? Perhaps the strongest argument against psychology moving into the territory of religion holds that religion itself, throughout history, has been an overflowing source of mental instability and violence, and that therefore it isn't appropriate for a rationally based would-be science to be too supportive of it. The Enlightenment, the intellectual foundation of science and modern society, came into being partly as a reaction against such irrational religious excesses as the Inquisition.

Is religion a destabilizing force? The institutionalized belief that Nancy Kehoe countered in creating religious discussion groups for the chronically mentally ill was that since it is known that "hyperreligiosity" is a tendency among psychotic patients, deliberately instigating religious thinking will inflame the delusions—will drive those hovering unsteadily on the border of sanity across to the other side. Kehoe's groups have contradicted this view, and in fact patients who have participated in her group discussions for long periods of time—including those with schizophrenia, bipolar disorder, and other serious conditions—have not only failed to see a renewal of their delusions but have felt better about themselves and their illness as a result.

Kehoe's work does not necessarily contradict the notion that religion can lead to violence, that there is a seed of disorder embedded in the human religious impulse. It does, however, suggest that context is important. If it is a free, nondoctrinaire exchange of ideas, religious talk can be beneficial to a troubled mind. Terrorism doesn't spring from open-air discussions, but from closed rooms; *conspire* literally means "to breathe together," and in a close brotherhood of like minds individually held passions can get reechoed and amplified until they take on a reality of their own. Radical anti-abortionists feed and reinforce one another's sense of God-sanctioned violence.

The year before Salvi's attacks, Father David Trosch, a spokesman for militant anti-abortionists, wrote a manifesto promising that pro-choice advocates "will be sought out and terminated as vermin are terminated."[2] Outside Salvi's jail cell, the Reverend Donald Spitz, a Virginia anti-abortion leader, shouted through a megaphone, "We love you! Thank you for what you did in the name of Jesus!"[3] The militant anti-abortion fringe feels itself in a war with the larger society, and communicates through newsletters and Web sites that blend politics and religion, much as Islamic terrorists reinforce and encourage one another with political and religious ideology.

Psychiatrist and terrorism expert Frederick Hacker analyzed the problem of Irish terrorism this way: "Personality structure both reflects external conditions and creates them by projection of inner conflict. Witnessing and living the tragic spectacle of battling identities, nobody, least of all the Irish themselves, can tell whether the Irish problem is really religious, national, economic, personal, or all of these."[4]

As Hacker says, religion is not the only force behind these terrorists; economics and politics—feeling financially trodden, culturally threatened—matter as well. But we can allow ourselves to forget about the underlying religious motivation for precisely the reason that to take such a thoroughgoing ends-justify-the-means view of religion is so foreign to most of us. Is it possible that religious feeling—the feeling of oneness with others, of being swept up into the current of cosmic love and eternal goodness—has an element of violence in it? Of course it does. It is an avenue of human expression, and so will carry whatever baggage people choose to take with them as they travel down it. In the end, the "religion leads to violence" argument falters; you might just as easily say that education leads to violence since there is so much violence in schools. One might counter the argument by borrowing a slogan from the National Rifle Association: Religion doesn't kill, people do.

The argument does, however, help to define the range of religious manifestations. Add to Nancy Kehoe's findings the wealth of medical statistics that David Larson has marshalled, all of which show that faith correlates with health, and a strong case is made for what might be called healthy religiosity (William James talked about "the religion of healthy-mindedness"), which promotes life and health and with which psychology can ally itself. On the other side of the argument, Paul Duckro at the St. Louis Behavioral Medicine Institute has led studies on "scrupulosity" among religious professionals and found a high incidence of obsessive behavior—from never-ending praying to the Pontius Pilate handwashing syndrome—that correlates with religious observance. There would seem to be a continuum of behavior from scrupulosity on up to religion-fueled terrorism—call it the spectrum of unhealthy religiosity.

The psyche-spirit movement brings a particular sensibility to dealing with these negative manifestations of religion and may have something new to add to the debate about religious violence. For society as a whole, the easy way out of grappling with the issue is to make an a priori determination that any vicious, violent act is by definition not religious in nature. What is it, then? Mental illness, of course. *They're all crazy.* But a psychospiritual perspective demands that we examine the issue more closely; it asks that we take militant fanatics partly on their own terms. Whether to refer to John Salvi as mentally ill or suffering from unhealthy religiosity might seem a question of semantics, but the distinction matters. Would Shannon

Lowney and Lee Ann Nichols, the two young women who died at his hands, still be alive if, before he picked up his rifle on that day in 1995, Salvi had seen a psychiatrist who was sensitive to his religious needs?

Perhaps *any* psychiatrist might have helped, and might have averted tragedy, but a patient with a view of reality so totally based on a religious paradigm might also do better with a doctor who could talk the talk, who saw spiritual issues as important. "Radical respect" is psychiatrist Tony Stern's term for the ideal attitude he tries to bring to therapy. Any psychiatrist begins a relationship by first trying to ascertain whether a patient is dangerous, and if so will take whatever steps— medication, hospitalization—might be necessary to defuse the danger. And, moving to the next phase of treatment, any good psychiatrist will respect the patient's belief system. The difference between respect and radical respect is in how far the psychiatrist is willing to go in acknowledging the good in a patient's character and ideology. "The Talmud says, 'Learn from every man,' " said Stern. "That even includes religious terrorists. They have a tribalistic intensity that we all have somewhere inside, and many of us have lost touch with. That fire is necessary at times to torch through the layers of false comfort and spiritual lassitude within ourselves. I think most of us could use some of that willingness to sacrifice for a higher cause."

Stern does not advocate accepting such a person's worldview, but he tries to locate the core of it that he can appreciate as valid: "Anyone who says they have communicated with the divine, I assume they may have, but at the same time it's doubtful that they got the message completely clearly." Ideally, this open-ended respect translates into the patient having more respect for the doctor, and, perhaps, being open to dialogue, introspection, and change.

Having opened up a trust in the patient, such a doctor might then be in a better position to tease out the wishes and fears, the secret hurts and resentments that may lie beneath. Indeed, a spirit-sensitive psychology can shed light on the whole question of why people kill in the name of God. For example, one of the "eternal truths" that Paul Fleischman isolates—areas where religion and psychoanalysis overlap— he calls "witnessed significance." We all need to be seen to matter—we need it so much that to be denied it can lead to madness. We need to be appreciated, to be identified and extolled as unique and worthy. "Look at me!" the child constantly cries to the parent. "Hear my prayer, O Lord," begs the psalmist, who then goes on,

> Do not hide your face from me,
>   or I shall be like those who go
>   down to the Pit.
> Let me hear of your steadfast love
>   in the morning,
>   for in you I put my trust.
> Teach me the way I should go,
>   for to you I lift up my soul.[5]

All religions, Fleischman says, serve the need for witnessed significance, and psychoanalysis does as well: "[T]he years of spontaneous confession available through free association to an attentive listener provide the sense that one's inner life is of interest, importance, and significance."[6] This universal hunger, Fleischman goes on to say, provides "one explanation of why out-groups, political and religious minorities, and neglected social fragments frequently turn to religious fanaticism to satisfy one of their fundamental needs. The fantasy of being the favored intimates of a divine eye provides the very ingredient that their normal lives lack."[7] In talking to the psychiatrist hired by his defense attorneys, John Salvi complained as much about the Catholic Church refusing to listen to him as about the supposed anti-Catholic conspiracy. He considered himself an ardent Catholic who went to church and went to confession: "Whatever the Pope believes, I believe," he said.[8] On the other hand, Catholics were "sheep," Catholics were "silly. . . . Let me explain what silly is. Silly is we all sit there in church and we don't look at each other and we don't talk to one another." The Catholics allowed themselves to be financially persecuted; the Catholics "aren't a bright group of people. . . . If every Catholic was like me, just like me, the Catholic Church would have anything it wanted. . . . If every Catholic was like me their standard of living would be excellent. They would all have good jobs. They would all have what they need." If "each and every one of the Catholic people" would only "read what I want to tell them . . . we could wipe out the Antichrist."

On the Christmas Eve preceding his killing spree, Salvi stood at the back of his church listening agitatedly to the sermon; when it was finished and the priest said, "Jesus loves you," Salvi suddenly marched to the front and, with his horrified family members looking on, shouted, "Jesus doesn't love you!" and began a ranting lecture on the need for Catholics to defend themselves. "You are all fucking pussies!" he shouted as parishioners dragged him away. Whatever else was at work inside him, John Salvi seemed to be simultaneously withering and raging from a lethal lack of witnessed significance.

• • •

The religious cry for blood seems so alien to us that we prefer to think it only exists as an aberration, but it is as old as human sacrifice; it is consecrated in the symbol of the cross. The spectacle of tens of thousands of human beings, having abandoned the narrow slice of earth that is home to them, the one place where they might have some temporary warmth and respite from the wilds of disease and crime and early death, walking—*walking*—across Europe and into the sun-scarred, alien landscape of the Middle East in order to throw themselves murderously on an unknown army, all for the purpose of helping to wrest political control of the birthplace and death-place of Jesus from people who do not worship him as Christ—such a spectacle, such passion, simply closes down the modern mind; it is too fantastic to quite believe. But the Crusades went on for *two centuries*, and while, as with any war, historians enumerate many causes—newfound prosperity in Europe coupled with a suddenly rising birthrate translated into droves of adventurous young men in need of worlds to conquer—the force that heated the blood of these generations of holy warriors was otherworldly. When during the first Crusade its leaders became bogged down in establishing political control over towns their armies had conquered en route to Jerusalem, the common soldiery became so enraged that the holy goal they had signed on for was being forgotten that they settled the matter by burning the towns so that their masters would have nothing more to delay them. God hovered over the Crusade armies; visions, dreams, and miracles were as common and necessary a part of the Crusades as swords and tents.

Religion-fueled violence and terror is deeply woven into history, but perhaps out of an inability to quite comprehend it, we have tried to neuter it, to strip away the underlying spiritual motivation from much of it. Thus names for specific sects or eras associated with it have become depersonalized, turned into common nouns. We have taken the cross out of crusader; a zealot is no longer a member of a religio-political faction of Herodian Palestine but anyone with a bit too much fire in the eyes. The original berserkers were medieval Norse warriors who, sent far across the boundary of madness by religious fervor, would rape and murder indiscriminately and literally tear their enemies to pieces.

Girolamo Savonarola, the fifteenth-century Catholic terrorist/zealot/crusader, singlehandedly took on the Church and the Renaissance, instigating a pro-spirit and antimaterialistic terrorism that caught the Italian popular imagination for a brief period. During his regime in Florence humanistic thinkers were hunted down as enemies of God; heterodoxical books and articles of sensual clothing were collected and burned in enormous "bonfires of the vanities." All of this was a result of the monk's divinely inspired visions. It is tempting to undercut the spiritual interpretation of this near-dismantling of the Renaissance with a psychological one: "a pattern of pervasive distrust and suspiciousness of others . . . Quick to counterattack . . . May first become apparent in childhood and adolescence with solitariness, poor peer relationships, social anxiety . . ." (DSM-IV on paranoid personality disorder.) But strict psychohistory is rather passé these days. The original psychohistorian was Freud, and the original psychobiographical subject was Leonardo da Vinci. Why did the artist devote so much attention to that enigmatic smile in the *Mona Lisa?* Because, Freud concluded, it "awoke something in him which had for long lain dormant in his mind—probably an old memory." The memory, Freud speculated, was of the artist's endlessly loving and caring mother—but that overpowering love led to Leonardo's inability to have sexual relations, which in turn "caused him to sublimate his libido" and transform it into art.

Such straight-ahead interpretation and supposed revelation of underlying psychodynamics are frowned upon today as almost farcically speculative, but psychobiography as one component of biography is unavoidable, and even necessary. The psychiatrist Robert Coles has written that psychological profiling of historical figures is important "to connect the past with the present, to show with discretion how the application of a particular discipline, psychoanalysis, developed in the twentieth century, makes more intelligible to us events that had a different kind of coherence for others who lived long ago."[9] What is worth meditating on is the last part of that sentence: It is because these events "had a different kind of coherence" for those in the past that we can feel justified in using this modern tool to examine them. We simply can't know the way they knew; no matter how much we might try, the stuff of life will not hang together for us the way it did for them. At least, therefore, we can make these long-ago people more intelligible for us in our time, using the ways of knowing that have become second nature to us. A biography of the Emperor Constantine will almost inevitably touch on the influence that his strong-willed mother may have had on his conversion to Christianity and the Christianizing of the Roman Empire, but that will be only one gauge, along with the press of economic and political forces and how others of the time saw him and viewed his actions. Today we try to pile up as many different perspectives as we can in the belief that the disparate voices will form a chorus that, if not in harmony, will at least have power. Journalist Ron Rosenbaum's 1998 book *Explaining Hitler*, in which he gathers together dozens of different interpretations of the dictator's life and motivations, from psychosexual to theological to genealogical, and lets them reverberate off one another, epitomizes this trend.

This switching back and forth between several different theoretical magnifying glasses can be useful in the present as well, particularly with a life that seems alien to us, and at times *not* to do it can result in a disastrous misreading. What might have happened at Waco had the FBI and Alcohol, Tobacco and

Firearms agents made an effort to study David Koresh, the messianic leader of the Branch Davidian cult, in psycho-spiritual terms? They would have realized that a raid on the group's compound was exactly the wrong action to take against a cult that modeled itself on biblical communities who shut themselves off from and armed themselves against a world they perceived as evil and threatening. Biblical scholar Robert Funk analyzed the situation shortly after it ended, with eighty people dead: "The FBI was competing with God. In the minds of Koresh and his associates, that was an uneven match. The cult would act only if God instructed it to do so; the FBI was not God. It is difficult for law enforcement agencies to compre-hend the fact that some citizens might regard their authority as circumscribed, limited, perhaps even of the devil."[10] Unwilling to study history—to consider fully the religious and histori-cal mold they were dealing with—government agents were forced to relive it: the disastrous raid, culminating in what may have been a suicidal bonfire, had a striking similarity to the Roman assault on the Jewish retreat at Masada in A.D. 73, at which every Jewish man, woman, and child died rather than submit to what they considered an authority that tried to sup-plant God.

Sympathetic psychohistory is a useful method for under-standing those at a distance—whether the distance is cultural or historic. But it is easier to do when the person we are trying to understand is safely in the past. We will accept that the Crusader's bloodlust was genuinely motivated by his passion-ate regard for Jesus Christ, and his Muslim foe's by his equal fervor for Allah. As the twentieth century recedes into history, we will allow that the common Japanese soldier fought World War II with the genuine conviction that it was a holy war, that he was fighting in the name of Emperor Hirohito, divine off-spring of the sun goddess.

But there are limits to this willingness to accept the other person's worldview, and as we get nearer our time our own psychological needs come into play. For people of the distant past we can magnanimously allow their spiritual fire, but what about the holy warriors who bombed the World Trade Center in 1993? It is possible to take such a people on their own terms—we can construct a picture of their religious state of mind—but we don't actually credit it; we don't stay with it; we don't even try to find a seed of truth in it. The act was morally wrong, so we dismiss the view of reality that fostered it. We have two choices on how to judge such a person: guilty of a crime (a legalism, but it carries moral weight) or mentally ill. Mental illness puts the person in a different category: we excuse him from the game that the rest of us are playing. The trial of such a religiously inspired terrorist is layered with moral and psychological issues. "The determination of sanity that decides a defendant's fate," according to Frederick Hacker, "is made not by disinterested parties, but by community representatives who have their own rational and irrational needs for safety, protection, and retaliation. If the community is not too frightened of the offenders and accepts the sincerity of their story, they are classified as mentally ill and treated accordingly. But if the nature of their acts makes them too scary or horrible, they are disbelieved, classified as criminals, and disposed of accordingly."[11] If the crime is heinous, our need to see it punished outweighs considerations of the person's psychological—or psychospiritual—state.

· · ·

Religious terrorism in our day may spring from the same cultural secularism that stripped the spirit out of psychology. When we discount a worldview that sees the universe in terms of heaven and hell in favor of one based on particle physics and astronomy, are we repressing a side of ourselves we are uncomfortable with? Are we ensuring that it will come back to haunt us?

That duality of worldviews was neatly illustrated in an exchange between John Salvi and Phillip Resnick, psychiatrist at Case Western Reserve University School of Medicine, during Resnick's psychiatric evaluation of the killer.[12] Resnick, as a psychiatrist for the defense, was attempting to determine whether Salvi had indications of psychosis, upon which to base a claim of mental incompetency to stand trial. In turning the tables and becoming the interrogator, Salvi, intentionally or not, showed the psychiatrist the narrowness of his—the psychiatrist's—worldview, and seemed to suggest that on this basic level he wasn't being listened to, and therefore, perhaps, help for him was impossible.

"Okay, Mr. Salvi, let me finish up a couple of other questions I wanted to get to," Resnick said. "Have you ever experienced any hallucinations?"

"No."

"Or heard voices talking to you, other people . . . ?"

"Never."

"Or seen visions other people didn't see?"

"No," Salvi said, and then asked, "Have you ever?"

"No." A moment later the psychiatrist asked, "Do you have any special powers that ordinary mortals don't have?"

"Special powers," Salvi repeated, and seemed to turn the phrase over in his mind. "Do *you* have any special powers that ordinary mortals don't have?"

"No," said the doctor.

"I don't believe I have," said Salvi, and then went on the offensive: "Let me ask you a question. Do you believe in faith healing?"

"In a sense," said Resnick. "[I believe] that there's a great power of, if someone psychologically believes someone can heal them, [that] can go a long way toward healing them. In that sense I do."

"Psychological power," said Salvi, specifying the kind of power that the psychiatrist meant. "You don't actually believe in *power*. What force controls atoms, Mr. Resnick?"

"Well, I see that you'd be glad to reverse roles here and conduct the interview," said Resnick. "But I don't think that's the most productive way I can spend my time here."

"Why?" Salvi replied. "I asked you a question. That's rude, right? I'm willing to answer most of the questions you asked me. Could you answer one I'm asking you?"

"I'll answer one. Okay."

"Okay, good. What power controls atoms? What force causes them to spin?"

"I don't even know the answer to that," said Resnick. "There's something called Brownian motion, is my understanding. But I don't know the physics of it enough to answer better than that."

"Okay," said Salvi. "So you don't believe in the power of a force, maybe a spirit, something that we don't know about, to heal?"

"Oh, I don't know the answer."

Having uncovered his interrogator's basic belief system, Salvi wanted to go further: "I'd like to know a little bit more about you. What religion do you belong to?"

Resnick declined to answer, and steered the interview back toward manifestations of psychosis. "Do you believe that you have the power to influence other people's minds, to influence their thoughts?" he asked.

"Do you mean as in a power like, I go like this and that affects you somehow chemically?"

"That would be one way."

"What about saying something that stimulates someone chemically? Everyone has the power to influence . . ."

"Everyone has the power of persuasion, sure, okay."

"I mean, it depends. When you bring up a suggestion, does that influence this individual? Everybody has that."

"Okay, I agree with you," Resnick conceded, and gave up on his line of questioning.

Salvi may been playing games with his interrogator— even though this was an utterly vital interview that would help to determine the young man's fate, his madness could have short-circuited all sense of practicality. But still, this conversation seems to show, rising up through the surface of the illness, bizarrely shaped flowers of thought that suggest a substratum composed of an entirely different type of soil. Here, in Salvi and the psychiatrist, were two different ways of seeing reality. Can we really say that Salvi's perspective is *wrong*? We condemn his action, of course, and shake our heads at his conspiracy delusion, but beneath all of that there seems to exist a kind of spiritual paradigm of the universe. One could imagine a Christian or Jewish mystic gently and playfully turning the interviewer's questions back on him in a similar way, or a Zen master fiercely confronting and unsettling the interview.

Many psychospiritual disorders, psyche-spirit practitioners seem to believe, have as much to do with society as with the individual. In Salvi's case, we unilaterally condemn the murderer's action, but if we had had the self-confidence to acknowledge his universe of belief—not the delusional system but the underlying spiritual commitment and passion—if, in other words, society had *listened* to him, would he have killed?

The world would surely be a better place if an answer to that question could be found. Perhaps someday the psyche-spirit movement will provide one.

John Salvi was found competent to stand trial, was convicted of murder, and sentenced to life in prison. In 1996, he was found dead in his cell, an apparent suicide.

9

The Walking Symbol

Pray without ceasing. . . .

—1 Thessalonians 5:16

"There are cases," Martin Buber once told the American psychologist Carl Rogers, when a psychologist must "help a man against himself. . . . What he wants is a being not only whom he can trust as a man trusts another, but a being that gives him now the certitude that 'there *is* a soil, there *is* an existence. . . . The world *can* be redeemed. I can be redeemed because there is this trust.' "[1]

There you have a précis of the kind of help that John Salvi did not receive. Buber was not talking about religious terrorists per se but broadly about anyone at war against himself, however public or private the struggle. The help he has in mind he calls confirmation, and by this he does not mean simply accepting the other person, or approving of the person's desires, but rather taking the whole person seriously—his beliefs, his worldview, his potential to grow. Confirmation may involve argument, real confrontation, but the confrontation takes place at least partly on the patient's terrain—inside the patient's world. In this way a soul in danger of dissipating can be grounded and helped to health. "There is not, as we generally think in the soul of man, good and evil opposed," Buber said. "There is again and again in different manners a polarity, and the poles are not good and evil, but rather *yes* and *no*, rather acceptance and refusal. And we can strengthen, or we can help him strengthen, the one positive pole. And perhaps we can even strengthen the force of direction in him because this polarity is very often directionless. It is a chaotic state. We could bring a cosmic note into it."[2]

If good and evil can be seen in terms of yes and no, of acceptance and refusal, then the moral forces at work in psychotherapy and religion are the same—the psychotherapist can bring "the cosmic note." "The good," Buber said, "is always only direction. Not substance." If that is so, changing moral direction does not require a supernatural alchemy but a true companion, someone who will "confirm the other," who will pay radical respect.

Confirmation, radical respect, witnessed significance—that is what David Lukoff provided for Joshua Beil. It is what Nancy Kehoe provides for her groups of mental patients. It is precisely what John Salvi did not receive. But it does not require someone with a Ph.D. in psychology to bring about. If psychiatry and psychology are only now coming to recognize that the emotional territory overlaps the spiritual, others have long been aware of it, and have helped sick people by confirming the existence of their spiritual landscapes.

Marion Davis is sixty-two years old, has been diagnosed with schizoaffective disorder, and has been in psychiatric treatment since 1965. Her illness takes an overtly religious form, but the psychiatrists she has seen through the years have been traditional, not interested in venturing across the standard biomedical boundary. She has seen a marked improvement in her illness over the past few years, which came in two stages. The most recent was when she began taking a new antipsychotic medication, but she began to feel better before that, and she identifies her turnaround with a minister who specializes in helping people with severe mental illness, and who brings his own kind of radical respect to the task.

Early in life Marion Davis was smart, capable, and ambitious. She was class valedictorian in high school and graduated from college with a perfect 4.0 grade point average. She met Gerald, her future husband, in college; they married on the day of her graduation. Both were devout members of the Disciples of Christ Church, a Protestant denomination that blends a biblical approach to life with a lively intellectual tradition; both entered graduate school with the idea of eventually becoming missionaries for the church. Two children were born; the church sent the family to Brussels to learn French preparatory to an assignment in the Congo, but war in that part of Africa changed the plan and instead they were posted to northern Rhodesia.

The planning was not the best. "I loved being there," Marion said. "The experience was a treasure. But I could never do anything besides look after our two little kids. I had expected to work with the African women, but the teachers at the center were Africans and they could do a better job than I could." A complicating factor was that their son had been born mildly retarded and as he got older personality problems emerged. "He was hyperactive, a total nightmare, and it brought our family to the brink of destruction. One of the prayers I prayed was 'God help me to love this unlovable child.' He could not respond to us, to any kind of normal family love. He was like a wild animal."

The family moved back to the States after two years in

Africa, and set up a home in St. Louis. Marion had suffered a series of small physical and emotional ailments since the time she finished college. She now became more and more passive and let her outgoing husband make family decisions and lead their social life. She developed a feeling of worthlessness; she became convinced she had failed God by not succeeding as a missionary: "I didn't feel I had anything to offer anyone."

Then they met a couple with children about the same age, and as they began socializing with them something changed inside her. She didn't understand it at first because she had never felt it before, but finally it dawned on her that she was powerfully attracted to the man. "He would draw me out and talk with me. He knew how to find something in me that I didn't know was there. He found some value. Nobody had ever done that before. I had never experienced a sexual attraction before."

As soon as she realized what was happening, she met with the man, told him of her feelings, and told him that because of them she could not see him again. The next day she had a catatonic breakdown. "I was frozen still for several hours, standing in place. I felt like I was a lighthouse. I knew what was going on around me—the windows were open, the lights were on, the children were crying for me to pay attention to them. But I just stood there." Eventually she collapsed on the floor. When her husband came home he called an ambulance.

"That was the beginning of my mental problems," Marion said. "I couldn't face losing the one person who understood me." So began a lifetime of fluctuation between periods of normalcy and mental breakdown. She never had another catatonic episode, but her life has been crippled by a long cycle of manic and depressive spells. The hallmark of her manic illness is prayer; that is not to say that she prays for relief from the illness, but that prayer *is* the illness. "When I become ill I feel completely enveloped in God. I literally cannot stop praying. It totally rules my life." She prays for friends, for family members, for strangers. "I will see strangers in the street and begin praying, 'Please God be with them in any way that they need.'"

She speaks of the illness in medical terms, but also in theological ones. The state is "joyous," "ecstatic." "I feel God's presence when I'm ill. It is an exhilarating experience to feel that I'm following, every minute of the day, what God wants me to do and be. It's hard for me to want to get better because it is this miraculous thing. It feels good, even though I know that I'm in the midst of an illness. And I know there is evil involved as well, but it is hard to let go."

Interestingly, she uses the same term for her illness that Pam Williams uses in reference to the sexual abuse her older brother put her through. "I call it training. I feel that these periods of illness are training fields that God put me through, and they give me an insight that I would not have otherwise. The training is learning to give thanks for every blessing, even the simplest of things. That is just so important." The training is very demanding: "It completely takes over my day. I don't make dinner. I don't clean or take care of myself."

The illness has a potentially dangerous side as well. When an episode is coming on, she is liable to feel God commanding her to do certain things: to leave doors unlocked, to stop taking her medication, to drive recklessly. "I know some of this is not God talking. There's a mix of good and evil, and it's hard for me to distinguish when I'm in the middle of it."

Marion has had favorable opinions of most of the succession of psychiatrists who have treated her over the years, but none ever did better than keep her in the seesaw of illness and relative wellness, and they saw the praying as nothing more than the manifestation of an organic illness. "Keep it to a minimum," was the counsel of one. Her most recent psychiatrist, who changed her medication so that she began to see some real improvement in her condition, has been particularly uninterested in her religious explanations. "I told him these periods of illness are training grounds, that they teach me how to be thankful, that it all comes from God. He wouldn't accept that."

At about that time, the Rev. Timothy Carson, pastor of her Disciples of Christ church, began calling on her. Carson is a tall, straight-backed native of Kansas City with a gentle voice and an unflappable disposition. Seen in his church, resplendent in his robes of office, surrounded by imposing gray stone walls and polished wood, his admiring parishioners seemingly moneyed and educated, the whole church set in leafy acreage in a well-to-do suburb, Carson seems the embodiment of religion in its institutional guise: rational, sober, orderly. But from the time he became a minister of the church he felt himself drawn to the dark, irrational underside. He has become known in St. Louis for his work with people in the grips of psychosis and paranoia.

"People who have seen visions or had near-death experiences hear about me. They know that I do not consider such things as psychopathological. Also, I don't charge—I'm not a paid psychotherapist. They'll come to me. They always preface it: 'I've never told this to anyone else.' They tell you about an experience and then look at you, waiting for you to think they're crazy."

In providing this blend of theological and psychological counseling, Carson works in a distinguished tradition, one that has paralleled the rise and dominance of the Freudian and biomedical models in psychology. In 1923 a shy and nervous Presbyterian minister in Massachusetts named Anton Boisen was struck by a psychotic episode in which he became convinced of "a coming world catastrophe" and believed that "I myself was more important than I have ever dreamed of being."

He attempted suicide, believed that he would die and be resurrected, believed that "I really was acting in obedience to a divine command." In his subsequent stay in a mental hospital he found that he fell into a gap between the kinds of help provided by psychiatrists and clergy: "The doctors did not believe in talking with patients about their symptoms, which they assumed were rooted in some organic difficulty" while "the ministers from the neighboring village . . . might know something about religion, but certainly knew nothing about our problems."[3]

Boisen recovered, and made it his life's mission to bridge this gap between the theological and medical worldviews by schooling ministers in the science of mental disorder. In 1925 he led five theological students to a mental ward to study "living human documents" of psychospiritual distress. That was the beginning of the pastoral counseling movement, which has since spread around the world. Seminaries now routinely offer courses in psychology and medicine.

In fact, the movement probably succeeded too well. As the British pastoral counselor John Foskett writes, the balance between medicine and religion has shifted radically: "When a fourteenth-century Pope put out a contract on his physician, religion was in the driving seat. Now Christians are likely to be ingratiating themselves with modern medical men and women. The contemporary Christian healing movement . . . often uncritically adopts the curative stance of medicine."[4] Robert Coles tells the wrenching story of visiting a friend in the hospital who was dying of cancer. The man was a devout Catholic. A priest had just come to his bedside and talked about "stress," "coping," and "feeling." Afterward, the man was furious. "He had wanted to talk with the priest about God and His ways," Coles wrote, "about Christ's life and death, about the Gospel of Luke (a particular favorite), about Heaven and

Hell—only to be approached repeatedly with psychological words and phrases. In their entirety those words and phrases constituted a statement, an insinuation: you are in psychological jeopardy, and that is what I, an ordained priest of the Holy Roman Catholic Church, have learned to consider more important than anything else, when in the presence of such a person as you."[5]

Tim Carson agrees that psychologizing has become problematic in his field. "If you sit with a group of pastors today, they speak in psychological language like everyone else—complexes, repressions. We live in a psychological world, and many of them have become swallowed up in that." This was not what Anton Boisen had in mind in the 1920s. Consciously adopting the framework of William James, he believed that "a critical study of the inner world of thought and feeling and volition, as it is revealed to us in the great crisis experiences . . . may also contribute something to our understanding of man's nature and destiny." The experiences of Joshua Beil, Marion Davis, and others support Boisen's observation that "most persons in these periods of crisis feel that their eyes have been opened to unsuspected meanings and possibilities in their life. The so-called normal range of vision becomes for them inadequate and superficial."[6]

Tim Carson has not succumbed to the lure of biomedical reductionism. In his freelance, voluntary counseling of parishioners and others with serious mental disturbances he adopts many of the same views about the intertwining of mental illness and spirituality that practitioners in the psyche-spirit movement hold. "I recently visited with a woman in the midst of multiple crises. From a psychological perspective we talk about what coping method she might use, and her degree of anxiety. From a spiritual standpoint we wonder what her level of trust is in God, what spiritual resources she is drawing on.

You can ask all those questions, and that's the exciting thing about this time. We've gone beyond the time when we thought it had to be either-or, that you have to think psychologically or religiously."

If a man with schizophrenia believes his hallucinations and delusions have a religious component, "I'll go with him there. I deal with the images that come up in dreams and visions, with the symbols exhibited during an episode." Carson's orientation is a mixture of Jungian psychology and the religio-anthropological work of Mircea Eliade, Emile Durkheim, and Victor Turner. Mental illness puts someone in a "liminal state," an in-between state, outside the rational world, outside roles defined by family, career, and society, outside even concepts of time and space. That is also the place of religious experience, and many traditional societies treated those who entered this place in religious terms. "Though their experience might be described as psychotic within certain schools of thought," Carson has written, "it is not at all to be considered psychopathological within the culture in which it is found; quite to the contrary, their culture venerates them because of the psychic journeys in which they have participated, and from which they draw their spiritual depth and authority."[7] Carson follows Michel Foucault, who, in his 1988 book *Madness and Civilization*, argues that madness is determined by society, not by some universal standard. Foucault documents a shift in attitude in the West beginning in the seventeenth century, the time of the Enlightenment and the rise of science. As rationalism and the biomedical model became dominant, liminal experiences lost their sacred character and were pathologized.

In the 1970s an international anthropological study was made of artwork created by people in the midst of psychotic episodes. The subjects were from several Western countries as well as New Guinea. The anthropologists found that the more profound the psychosis, the more alike the subjects' art became, no matter where they were from.[8] Carson sees this as evidence of a Jungian collective unconscious, a primordial pool of meaning that all humans share. Those who descend into it are labeled prophetic or mad, according to the dictates of their culture. "In the past, people called that deep common pool 'God,' and they accessed it through religious rites and traditions," he said. "Now we call it by different names. It's like we're all hovering at the top of a well and looking down into it. It's where we all drink."

Carson believes psychotic states have a "transformational power" if they are ridden out rather than aborted, and so he devotes a great deal of his time and energy to helping such people. He holds with Anton Boisen, who wrote that psychotic delusions "may be looked upon as extreme manifestations of the consciousness of sin which theology has long regarded as the first step in the process of salvation. Like the fever and inflammation in the body, such disorders seem to be the manifestations of nature's power to heal."[9] "I'm a spiritual guide," Carson said. "You have to be willing to go with them on the journey. It takes a lot out of you, but it is extremely stimulating."

It is particularly stimulating when the results are good. Mark, one young man he saw—highly intelligent and from a solid family—had recently finished college and was about to start his first real job when "dreamy reality began pouring in." These spells of losing touch with ordinary life became more and more frequent; Mark agreed to Carson's offer of help. At the climax of the psychosis Mark "fully identified with the figure of Jesus Christ." He believed that he was suffering the sins of the world, that he was in direct communion with his Father, that his duty was to endure terrible suffering so as to bring about the redemption of the world. All of this, he later insisted, he knew with absolute clarity. With Carson's assistance, Mark came through the episode. It has become the experience that he measures all other things by.

"The frightening thing is you don't know it's going to be temporary," said Carson. "You're standing on the edge. You don't know if it's going to be life-giving or life-destroying." Larry, an educated, technically minded young man, was working as an engineer on a merchant marine freighter when, far out at sea, he was engulfed by a psychotic episode. *He was God.* He controlled not only the ship but the sea and the planet. His power was terrifying, it was overwhelming. He tried to persuade the captain that the ship had a destiny, that the captain and officers should henceforth follow his instructions.

Larry had no history of mental illness, but he did have a troubled childhood. Once he was back home, Carson stayed with him through the psychosis. The episode passed, but it proved to be the onset of a long-term condition. There have been other episodes since then, frightening experiences that have robbed him of his ability to get along in the world or to see himself as a complete person. "I would define his case as an illness, not revelatory," said Carson. "There is nothing redemptive in it."

In accompanying psychotics on their journey, Carson is doing what David Lukoff and others do. But he believes there is a crucial difference: Carson remains a man of the cloth. The pastor—or rabbi, lama, or imam—is a walking symbol. In Jungian terms, he is the manifestation of the archetype of the spirit, which confronts one at critical junctures of life. Such archetypal symbols make up the very language of the unconscious. A clergyman who "goes on the journey" with a sufferer thus has a potent advantage over a therapeutic professional. This is why, in Carson's view, ministers who replace a theological worldview with a psychological one are doing a disservice:

they relinquish the real power to heal that comes with their office.

"I once entered the hospital room of a parishioner when he was having a full-blown psychotic episode and hallucinations," Carson said. "The devil and all his minions were in the room taunting him. I walked in, and I happened to be taking the communion to him that day. For him, communion is a genuine symbol. It is the body and blood of Christ. I came in, and he started laughing, and he said to the demons, 'Do you know who he is?' And then he pointed to the black box I was carrying and said, 'Do you know what's in there?' And I set the box on the table in front of him, and instantly the hallucinations were gone. Now you might say that a deep emotion overpowered all of the electrical impulses that were moving through his cerebrum, or, from a spiritual perspective, the power of his faith expunged everything that wasn't good."

Not everyone he sees, however, is a member of his church, or even a Christian. "If the person shares your symbol system, you talk that language—it has power that comes with it. If not, you find the language that the person does know. I find that even people who have not been raised in a religious tradition have a kind of implicit theology. Just being a minister is often enough to break down resistance. There's a built-in trust—they believe you probably are a person of goodwill."

Carson had been a friend as well as minister to Marion Davis and her husband. "When Tim came to see me in the hospital I told him I felt like these spells were religious experiences," Marion said. "I said I felt it was something good that was happening to me. These periods teach me how to be thankful. I told him that through them I was learning to pray for others, not just selfishly thinking about myself." Her psychiatrist had dismissed this, but "Tim listened."

"I did listen," Carson said. "With me she tried to sort out

what is healthy religion and what is unhealthy. She would get into some strange places where she felt she was being compelled to do dangerous things. She had to do some reality testing. She would share an experience and ask, 'Is this healthy?' "

Marion's compulsion to pray was more problematic. Many religious sects exalt the idea of "ceaseless prayer." St. Paul instructed the Thessalonians to "pray without ceasing. . . . Do not quench the Spirit." *The Way of a Pilgrim*, a spiritual text of the Eastern Church written by an anonymous nineteenth-century Russian pilgrim, which has been reprinted in many editions in recent years, advocates unending prayer as a way of life. "The Jesus Prayer"—which consists of the line "Lord Jesus Christ, Son of God, have mercy on me, a sinner"—is to be uttered with every breath, the first half on the inhale and the second on the exhale. In time, it becomes more than second nature for the pious persons who carry it out; they "become" the prayer; it prays them.

In *The Varieties of Religious Experience*, William James quotes Auguste Sabatier, a French theologian, on prayer: "[P]rayer is real religion. It is prayer that distinguishes the religious phenomenon from such similar or neighboring phenomena as purely moral or aesthetic sentiment. Religion is nothing if it be not *the vital act by which the entire mind seeks to save itself by clinging to the principle from which it draws life. This act is prayer. . . .*"[10] The phrase that I have highlighted seems to sum up Marion Davis's illness. Anyone who has spent time with her during one of her episodes would assert that it is indeed an illness from which she suffers, and yet something about it *fits the very definition of religion.* Prayer is a bridge to the divine, the connecting tissue between the individual and the All. To feel compelled to pray constantly, to the exclusion of all else, is surely crippling, but is there also a sense in which it is genuinely liberating? Is the way out of such an illness perhaps to work through it? Surely the psychiatrist who advised her—for twenty-five years—to "keep it to a minimum" was avoiding the genuine theological aspect of her illness. "Prayer does not demand that we interrupt our work," said Mother Teresa, "but that we continue working as if it were a prayer."[11]

"Certainly there is a strong spiritual dimension to Marion's need to pray," Carson said. "And there are of course worse conditions than to constantly want to be in touch with God. But, to me, when it inhibits your functioning in the world, you cross a line." Volition is one of Carson's catchwords; the difference between a mystic and someone with mental illness is that the former can choose to move into or out of the state.

This is a point of argument among those in the psyche-spirit movement, a matter of definition. How does one definitively distinguish between religious experience and pathology? David Lukoff and Tomás Agosin both developed ways to determine if someone was in contact with the divine or merely confused. For Agosin, the defining characteristic of genuine religious experience was selflessness: where a delusional person will become inflated and grandiose in the state, a mystic feels his or her individual identity shrink so as to become almost beside the point. Marion Davis passes this test—in the midst of an episode she remains meek, almost subservient—yet Carson still believes her condition contains an aspect of illness as well as of piety.

There has been one scientific study done comparing reported mystical experiences of religious contemplatives and psychotics. In 1993, researchers at the Southern Virginia Mental Health Institute and the pastoral counseling department of Loyola College gave psychiatric tests to three groups of people: thirty people diagnosed with psychosis who had exhibited hyperreligiosity; thirty senior members of contemplative religious orders; and thirty members of the general public. One of the tests given was the Hood Mysticism Scale, an instrument developed in 1975 that identifies such features of the experience as feelings of "ineffability, spatiotemporal perceptual alteration, numinosity, positive affective states" and "absorption of the self into a larger whole." On this test, the scores of the contemplatives and the psychotics were indistinguishable from one another, but were markedly different from those of the "ordinary" group. On two personality tests, however, which measured narcissistic tendencies and "ego-grasping," or the need to control one's environment, the contemplatives and the "ordinary" group scored almost identically, while the psychotic group rated notably higher in narcissism and ego-grasping. The results, according to the authors of the study, "lend tentative support to the theoretical position that considers mystical experience in psychosis, and mystical experiences within varying religious traditions, to be essentially the same, with only minor differences due to cultural expectation and verbal interpretation." There is, however, a marked difference between mystics and psychotics in terms of "personality structure and maturity."[12]

In terms of the experiences themselves, then, this study supports the idea that if the mystic's experience is to be called religious then so too should the psychotic's. Perhaps the real differences are exterior to the persons involved: *we* prefer to think of one as religion and the other as mental illness; we prefer the idea that religion brings well-being and control. We prefer to think of real religion as something that we choose to engage in, not something that forces itself upon us. So we make an arbitrary determination: *this* is religion, *that* is mental illness masquerading as faith.

Or, if we allow that our psyches and our souls are inextricably woven together, we can refer to the two states as healthy and unhealthy religiosity. We can acknowledge the religious experience as genuine and at the same time give the person help with what might be a disturbed or immature "personality structure."

Tim Carson prefers a firmer distinction—that at some point Marion's condition crosses from religious experience to mental illness—but he acknowledges that his position is subjective. "This is just my way of looking at it. For example, some of Marion's religious experiences take her to what I would call irrational conclusions. God will tell her that she shouldn't lock her doors. Now, you could see that in a profoundly spiritual way she is wanting to open herself up to the whole world, even a world that includes evil. On the other hand, the practical side of me says she's going to get robbed."

More important, Carson did acknowledge the inner God–talk that was so fully a part of Marion's life; he, as her pastor, gave it theological confirmation, and that mattered a great deal to Marion. That they wrangled about how much of it was truly of God is in keeping with Buber's idea of confirmation, which does not mean simple acquiescence. God did indeed call Marion to prayer, and in so doing taught her "how to be thankful"; the inner voice encouraging her to pray helped her to see herself in relation to the infinite; it opened up a correspondence with the universe; it put her life in perspective. Having Carson agree with this helped to give her, in Buber's words, "the certitude that 'there *is* a soil, there *is* an existence. . . . The world *can* be redeemed.' "

They also had somewhat different interpretations of the dangerous directives Marion received. Marion believes in evil as an entity, one that in some way is bound up with God, and that the voice that goads her into danger is both evil and illness. Carson too believes in evil, but he reserves it for activity of another order entirely. "I am happy to exist in two places at once, in the psychological and the theological, but I tend to think there is a crossover, not a complete identity. I think there is a dimension of evil that transcends our psychologizing. What the Nazis did, the genocide that has taken place in the

Balkans—that goes beyond psychological mechanisms." On the smaller scale, Carson finds it more helpful to talk in medical and psychological terms than to take the "devil made me do it" escape.

As Marion's condition improved, her life took a series of turns that had the wrenching irony of tragedy—and Tim Carson's presence through this period illustrates some of the potential difficulty of being pastor as well as psychospiritual counselor. Throughout the decades of her illness, years of hospitalizations, and family turmoil, Marion's husband had remained patient and supportive—this despite the fact that her illness, and that of their son, had kept him from fulfilling his life's ambition to be a missionary. But as she felt better she began to look at herself in a new light. She saw herself as weak and passive and wracked by feelings of inferiority, and she took steps to change. She realized that while she was not a person of tremendous action, she was very good at being with people, at comforting others, and she became more involved with friends, her family, and at her church. In little ways, she was at last fulfilling her own missionary dream. In Tomás Agosin's Jungian terms, she was strengthening her ego so that it would no longer become lost in the Self.

The act of asserting herself also involved seeing her marriage from a new perspective. She realized how much her husband controlled her life: he determined who she saw, what she did. He reacted strongly to the changes. "Gerald could accept my illness, but he couldn't accept this. He loved me dearly— until I started to become my own person." She now believes that her thirty-six-year relationship with her husband played an important role in her illness; she and her husband had an arrangement that worked for both for many years, but it depended on her being debilitated and largely helpless. Marion also believes that Tim Carson, in his counseling of the couple, took her husband's side, and tried to convince her to go slower in changing so as to save her marriage. She couldn't, however, and came to feel that Carson was trying to retard her psychological growth.

Gerald, meanwhile, grew increasingly irritated with his newly self-assertive wife. "Things have to change or else," he would say, but he wouldn't say what things. Marion understood that in changing herself she was putting him through emotional turmoil, but she couldn't stop the process. Finally he asked for a divorce. She moved out of the house and into an apartment; they were divorced in 1993. The next year Gerald informed her that he was going to remarry. Marion was stunned but on some level not surprised by the news. Gerald was still reacting to the changes in her, trying to fill a void in his life.

Tim Carson performed the wedding service. The next day, Carson arrived unexpectedly at Marion's apartment, saying that he wanted to be the one to break the news to her. "What, didn't they get married?" she asked. He said they had, but that shortly after Gerald arrived home with his new wife he suffered a massive heart attack and died.

"I started to shake violently," Marion said. "I kept shaking for months." She has been hospitalized five times since Gerald's death and has spent long periods reliving the moments of their life together, feeling alternately deep love and a conviction that their relationship fed her illness.

There is no telling whether Marion would have climbed as far out of the trench of her suffering had she not known Tim Carson. Throughout her decades of interaction with psychiatrists not a single one was of a mind to consider that her illness might extend beyond the scope of medicine, but, as it happened, it didn't matter; she didn't need someone with a degree in psychology or medicine to connect her praying obsession to both her brain chemistry and her soul. A pastor could do the job, as Anton Boisen realized half a century before.

Such boundary crossing may come at a price, however. Marion remained bitter at Carson, whom she believed could not see that she had grown stronger but continued to think of her as seriously mentally ill and in need of supervision. Shortly after Gerald's death, she left his church.

. . .

The sad climax to Marion's married life makes one wonder about the many subterranean ways people are interconnected. William James believed that underlying our everyday view of ourselves as individuals is "an extended subliminal self" that merges us with those near to us and, ultimately, with God.[13] If Marion's mental illness is interwoven with her religious life, and if her own life was interwoven with her husband's, to what extent did he share her psychospiritual disorder? Thwarted from becoming a missionary, did he craft his wife's illness into his own cross, which allowed him to follow Jesus' example of suffering? Did her illness play a psychospiritual role in his life? Did it give him his own "imitation of Christ"?

"In a funny way, I think the illness was as much Gerald's as mine," Marion said three years after Gerald's death. "He made the illness his crusade in life: he developed a spouses' support group with the National Alliance for the Mentally Ill. When I began to get better it upset his balance." Gerald had had an ongoing heart condition, which Marion felt sure was related to stress. "He never dealt with his stress. He prided himself on being a caretaker, but he would never admit that *he* needed help. During our breakup he wound up in the hospital because of stress, and he was mortified to be in a psychiatric ward. To the very end, he needed to be in control. The strange thing was my illness helped me to grow, while Gerald, who always had to be so strong, never understood how weak he was."

Gerald's funeral gave Marion a slightly eerie glimpse of how much her "subliminal self"—illness, psyche, soul—had merged with his. Many people who lose a spouse after a long marriage speak of the death of a part of themselves. Tim Carson was to perform the funeral ceremony (just days after he had performed Gerald's marriage service), and so he asked Marion whether Gerald had any preferences for the service. She told him where in the house he could find papers they had drawn up indicating the prayers and other arrangements each would like for their respective funerals. "The funny thing was, Tim ended up using more of the prayers from my list than from Gerald's," Marion said. "So as I sat there listening to just the right music and just the right prayers, and feeling everything so much, it suddenly struck me—this is the closest I'm ever going to get to being at my own funeral."

10

Satan in the Brain

I do not make any clear distinction between mind and God. God is what mind becomes when it has passed beyond the scale of our comprehension.

—FREEMAN DYSON

[D]eliver us from evil. . . .

—MATTHEW 6:13

A house needs walls. A profession needs boundaries. There must be things that help us to say, "No, you have crossed a border here. You are in another territory." If the psyche-spirit movement has dedicated itself to tearing down one of the supporting walls of psychology—the idea of a distinct self—should it erect something else in its place? Presumably, what it gives us instead is an expanded self, a self that shades off into other selves, into society, eventually to dissolve, like a grain of spice, into the stew of the universe. The notion is lyrical, perhaps profound, but it also makes life more confusing.

Certain phenomena that have sprung into being within the field of psychology push this question to the fore. Over the course of the 1990s, for example, "Christian counseling" went from an obscure practice to an outright industry. Christian counselors are trained mental health professionals, but with a difference. "We use many of the same methods as secular therapists," said Gary Collins, president of the American Association of Christian Counselors. "We say mm-hmm. We build rapport. But we are also guided by Christian values. We might quote Scripture, or suggest that the person become involved in a body of believers. We might pray with the person." Many of these techniques are employed by other therapists in the psyche-spirit movement, and a pastoral counselor might use some of them as well; the difference is allegiance to—some would say promotion of—a specific religion. Particularly in its more strident forms, Christian counseling does not seek to correct an imbalance in traditional psychology but to *replace* it with a new psychology based on the precepts of a particular religion. (The pastoral counseling tradition, by contrast, has an ecumenical slant: a pastor such as Tim Carson works with a person's religious background, whatever it may be, and his work augments that of a secular doctor.)

While the AACC stresses that its members take a wide variety of approaches to their work, there is an underlying philosophy behind much of the Christian counseling movement. A column in the association's magazine, for example, outlines for Christian counselors how to use the Bible to lead homosexuals out of their "false self." ("[H]omosexuality is not essentially a sexual problem," writes psychologist Joseph Nicolosi, "but an identity problem characterized by a form of narcissism. . . . Authentic religious experience—the felt reality of God's presence in one's core being—obliterates narcissism.")[1] Some Christian counseling also contains a pronounced absolutist message. Stephen Arterburn, president of New Life Clinics, which the evangelical magazine *Christianity Today* has called "the nation's largest Christian psychiatric company," lists as one of the primary differences between Christian and secular counselors that "Christian counselors help people face the truth about themselves."[2] There is also a tendency to proselytize in the movement. Arterburn has written that part of a Christian counselor's job is to "help people focus on heaven. . . . As for those who have not accepted Christ, by making heaven a possibility, *the counselor is free to encourage them to do so* as long as he doesn't manipulate compliance or force acceptance."[3] (Emphasis added.) Arterburn does not say how it is possible for a counselor to encourage a therapy client to accept Christ and at the same time not manipulate him.

At the other end of the psyche-spirit spectrum are submovements such as the alien abduction phenomenon, which holds that alien beings have been visiting earth for centuries and commingling with humans, and that these encounters qualify as spiritual experiences. According to John Mack, the Harvard psychiatrist whose 1994 book *Abduction* gave the phenomenon mainstream attention, "The alien beings that abductees speak about seem to many of them to come from another domain that is felt to be closer to the source of being or primary creation. . . . As their experiences are brought into full consciousness, abductees seem to feel increasingly a sense of oneness with all beings and all of creation."[4]

Like Christian counseling, alien abduction is a wayward child (or godchild) of the psyche-spirit movement. As the walls of the psyche are pushed back, each of these areas declares that its spiritual truth is legitimate, even imperative. Both movements are taken very seriously in certain quarters. The American Association of Christian Counselors, for instance, began in 1991 with 700 members; by 1998, 15,000 mental health professionals belonged to it. Alien abduction is perhaps more peripheral, but it too has licensed practitioners who, in the words of one, "specialize in helping people process and integrate" encounters with alien beings.

Finding responsible critics who take exception to this sort of psychology is not difficult, but that isn't the point. Robert

Spitzer, a Columbia University psychiatry professor and former chairman of the DSM task force, said of Mack, "It's a little embarrassing that a psychiatrist from a prestigious university believes in the reality of those experiences, but what can you do about it?" Indeed, what can the field do about it? The point is that, whether one finds Mack's argument about alien abduction convincing or not, it is a challenge to the profession, one that bears directly on the spiritual opening up of the psychological professions. Why *shouldn't* alien abduction be given as much credence as virgin birth stories or resurrection claims? If communications with Jesus or the Hindu elephant god Ganesh are legitimate, why discriminate against the flying saucer crowd?

And if some Christian counselors believe that Jesus is the one and only way, and that therefore they have a moral imperative to mix the gospel of Jesus Christ into their prescriptions, to preach while they practice, why shouldn't they do so? Nonsectarian psyche-spirit practitioners may assert that proselytizing is against the rules, but how do they counter what some believe is a higher authority?

These are difficult questions. When moving into the realm of the nonrational, it is hard to define rational boundaries. The psyche-spirit movement began with a seemingly harmless notion, that letting "soul" be part of "self" would be a good, healthy, productive course for the human sciences to follow. But with such vocal and often strident armies camped on opposite flanks, truth seems more elusive than ever. Can we find a way to sort through these competing truth claims?

One possibility is to examine the whole psyche-spirit movement at the laboratory level. What hard, scientific evidence is there, after all, to support any part of the migration into the spiritual realm by this field? Perhaps by locating it, we might find a way to begin sorting out reasonable and unreasonable spirituality.

Consider Margaret W. For thirty years Margaret lived with the firm conviction that she was Satan. It came on her in the mid-1960s, when she was about thirty years old. She had been hospitalized for severe depression, and while there read John Steinbeck's *East of Eden* and came across the following passage:

> I believe there are monsters born in the world to human parents. Some you can see, misshapen and horrible, with huge hands or tiny bodies; some are born with no arms, no legs, some with three arms, some with tails or mouths in odd places. They are accidents and no one's fault, as used to be thought. Once they were considered the visible punishments for concealed sins.
>
> And just as there are physical monsters, can there not be mental or psychic monsters born? The face and body may be perfect, but if a twisted gene or a malformed egg can produce physical monsters, may not the same process produce a malformed soul?[5]

It was like a revelation, a hideous revelation. "I suddenly knew it was true. I saw everything." *She* was such a malformed soul. Hers wasn't merely a wounded spirit, but a nonspirit, a nullity. And, as she settled deeper into this groove, she realized that even this dead-end notion of the soul was not sufficient to characterize her case; she was active evil, blackness thrusting itself into the world.

She reviewed her life and saw the indications. What she had formerly thought were slights she had committed against friends or family members were in fact tentacles of evil: "I began to see everything in diabolical terms." She fixated on the Holocaust, which had taken place during her childhood and had always fascinated her, and the conviction dawned that she had caused it. It wasn't a matter of being a bad person; it was "being outside God's provenance." It was being "not human, a subhuman entity." She slowly came around to facing the black hole of truth: "I was the devil for thirty years," she says today. For those thirty years she lay chained to her bed—not literally, but the shackles were real; they weren't chains of fear so much as of deadness. Keeping herself as close to death as possible was the only solution. She was a prisoner of her Satan-self; she had no life.

Today Margaret lives outside Boston in a halfway house for the mentally ill; she still suffers from bouts of depression, but the devil vanished suddenly five years ago. Her psychiatrists had tried many antipsychotic drugs on her over the years, but none had a pronounced effect until Risperdal came along. There was a short period before it took effect and then "one day I just said, 'What happened to the devil?' " In the depths of a depressive episode Margaret is still prone to think of herself as a bad person, but that is a far remove from the very pit of hell that she has climbed out of. "Now I might think of myself as a sinner, which is a very different thing. No matter how bad it gets, I know I'm within God's light."

Relieved of the horrific burden of being damned to hell, outside the light and life of goodness, Margaret has joined the human race. She works on the Human Rights Committee of the Massachusetts Department of Mental Health; she is active in her Episcopalian church; she has written for several publications about spirituality and mental illness. She still suffers from deep and chronic pain, which she describes as physical but more particularly psychospiritual, pain that can be so debilitating it can prevent her from functioning. She takes an antidepressant to ease it, but she has found that the best treatment is to start every day with another kind of medicine. Especially since the devil vanished, she has become enticed—intoxicated might be the right word—by mathematics. She begins her day with differential calculus, which she calls "abandonment." "I can't explain it," she said, "but calculus takes away the pain. I'm addicted to it." Calculus and prayer are twin forms of release; she relies on both, and although she is theologically a fairly conservative Christian, at times she isn't so sure that the mathematics and the prayer aren't the same thing.

Like most of the mental patients featured in this book, Margaret sees her illness in spiritual as well as medical terms. Unlike most, she believes religion may have played some role in the form her delusion took. Her parents were not religious, so it was not a part of her early life. In college she became interested in it, and, she says, applying religious terminology to herself became an obsession. "I had this focus on sin, which is okay as long as you are aware of God's forgiveness. I suppose it paved the way for the devil thing."

Because her condition—a psychospiritual condition if ever there was one—was changed so decisively by a drug, Margaret's case provides an opportunity to explore the biochemical-spiritual intersection. It's almost as if Risperdal flipped a switch; it changed her spiritual polarity, transported her from outside to inside the heavenly embrace.

Is there a "God center" in the brain, a place where the ineffable stuff of spirit—evil spirit or beneficent spirit—conjoins with human flesh? The question is tied to the so-called mind-body problem, which for centuries philosophers tried to solve by looking for an organ where the physical brain translates into a nonphysical mind. In the estimation of seventeenth- and eighteenth-century thinkers, this postulated nonphysical entity encompassed both mind and soul. It had to be nonmaterial because if the mind/soul were physical then it would presumably die with the body, which would violate Christian precepts. Descartes nominated the pineal gland, at the center of the brain, as the organ where this mysterious transformation occurred. He was wrong (the pineal gland is now known to be responsible for the production of melatonin, which regulates the wake-sleep cycle), and the primary reason for his error provides another warning of the dangers of venturing down this path. Whatever the mysterious force or material responsible might be, in Descartes's model it has somehow to be able physically to nudge the gland or organ that will translate its ineffable idea (pick up the chainsaw! dodge the falling tree!) into physical activity in brain and body. But if it has this capability, why can that interaction not be measured or monitored? If an eight ball is struck by a cue ball and caroms into a pocket, the laws of physics say the change in its trajectory must be traceable to a source of energy (the moving cue ball): the energy responsible for the eight ball's movement equals the energy expended by the cue ball as it struck. But if the ineffable thought is the cue ball and the brain activity is the eight ball, the ineffable thought must have expended energy in order to "strike" the brain, which would make it of the physical world, and thus not ineffable after all. In the terminology of physics, Descartes's theorized "ghost in the machine" (as Gilbert Ryle famously derided it) violates the law of the conservation of energy. The philosopher Daniel Dennett put it this way: "It is the same incoherence that children notice—but tolerate happily in fantasy—in such fare as Casper the Friendly Ghost. How can Casper *both* glide through walls and grab a falling towel? How can mind stuff *both* elude all physical measurement and control the body?"[6]

Dualism has stuck around because it makes a lot of common sense—it is the way we tend to imagine things to be. We may go along with the idea that thinking occurs by virtue of physical processes in the brain, but we have a hard time believing that the thoughts themselves are physical things. Conjure up a bizarre creature that doesn't exist in nature or anywhere else—a pig with gills, say. Do we really believe that this fleeting thought beast has some sort of physical presence in the brain? Or, to take an example from the more meaningful end of the spectrum, consider Yahweh, the God of Israel. Is a devout Jew willing to consider the possibility that the entity that goes with that name exists merely as neurochemical splashes in the brains of believers? For that matter, is such a person willing to believe that this entity has physical existence in some other realm or universe? In either case, thinking of Yahweh as a physical entity would be repellent to such a believer: the Lord God, one might hold, is more than that, more than mere matter.

Our ordinary thinking, then, whether on a trivial or profound matter, tends to be dualistic, but the approach of most contemporary scientists and philosophers dismisses Cartesian dualism (the belief that reality comprises two substances, material and mental/spiritual), as profoundly unworkable and forces one down other avenues of thought in an attempt to make sense of mind-body, body-soul conundrums. Some philosophers and scientists believe that solving the problem is a matter of refining our equipment, of building brain-scanning techniques even more sophisticated than functional magnetic resonance imaging, the current state of the art. One interesting line of thinking postulates that spirituality is an activity of the right hemisphere of the brain. The reasoning is mostly theoretical, although there is some research behind it as well. Lists of the features of a mystical experience, such as those compiled by Abraham Maslow and William James, all include "ineffability"—the experience is hard to put into words. Since language is almost exclusively an activity of the left hemisphere, as experiments with epileptics and others have shown, this would suggest that the experience takes place in the nonverbal hemisphere. Other identified features of the experience are the seeming nonexistence or distortion of space and time;

both spatial sense and time orientation are features of the right hemisphere. Also, while the left brain tends to analyze and break things down into constituent parts, the right brain has more of a capacity for seeing the big picture, for grasping and appreciating things as a whole, whether it is the beauty of a rose or the wonder of life.

If an experience occurred exclusively in the right brain, in other words, it would likely be hard to describe, would seem to exist outside the normal understanding of space and time, and would be perceived holistically rather than in pieces: precisely the characteristics of mystical experience.

Other studies of people with epilepsy seem to implicate the temporal lobes as a region of the brain where religious experience takes place. Throughout time, some people who have had epileptic seizures in the temporal lobe have reported, as part of the aura, or pre-seizure experience, feelings of joy, peace, and contentment. The example often pointed to is from Dostoevsky's *The Idiot*. Dostoevsky himself suffered from epilepsy, and the description is thought to be autobiographical: "[T]here was a moment or two in his epileptic condition . . . when suddenly amid the sadness, spiritual darkness, and depression, his brain seemed to catch fire . . . culminating in a great calm, full of serene and harmonious joy and hope, full of understanding of the final cause." British neuropsychiatrist Peter Fenwick reports that "it is not uncommon to find fragments of this experience in the epileptic aura" and suggests, "A standard question to ask a patient is whether, during their auras, they have spoken to God. It is surprising how often the answer is yes. These findings demonstrate . . . a link between psychosis and temporal lobe function and between temporal lobe function and mystical experience."[7]

An experiment conducted at the University of California at San Diego in 1997 also used epileptics to show that the tempo-

ral lobe plays a role in religious experience. The neuropsychiatrist Vilayanur Ramachandran tested a group of epileptics
who had temporal lobe seizures in which they reported mystical experiences, and found that they had an unusually
high emotional response to the mere mention of religious
terms (such as "God") compared to two control groups. The
results, said Ramachandran, suggest that "there may be
neural circuits in the temporal lobe that may be part of the
machinery of the brain that is involved in mystical experiences
and God."[8]

However, religious experience may not be a single entity but
instead encompass a range of states of consciousness, with a
corresponding range of brain activity. There was no indication
in the U.C. San Diego study that the right temporal lobe was
more active than the left. Another study, at the University of
Pennsylvania, used single positron emission computed tomog-
raphy (SPECT) to visualize the brains of Buddhist monks during meditation. The scanner revealed that as the meditation
deepened, activity in the parietal and frontal lobes of the brain
diminished. Since these areas are responsible for (among other
things) spatial orientation of the body, the thinking is that
diminished activity in these regions leads to the experience
during meditation of "being nowhere."

Zooming in from brain region to brain chemistry, Risperdal,
the drug that cured Margaret W. of the belief that she was the
devil, is one of the new generation of antipsychotics.* It, in
common with virtually all psychiatric drugs, acts on the chemicals in the brain called neurotransmitters. These chemicals
transmit signals between neurons, or nerve cells, in the brain by
jumping across the synaptic cleft between neurons and lodging
in the "receptor sites" of the adjoining neuron. There are many

---

*Risperdal, like Prozac, is actually a brand name; the drug itself is called risperidone.

types of neurotransmitters, but the best known are dopamine and serotonin. Most antipsychotic drugs block dopamine receptor sites; most antidepressant drugs block serotonin receptor sites, and so cause a buildup of serotonin in the synaptic cleft. Antidepressants such as Prozac are thus called serotonin reuptake inhibitors. The common understanding has been to think of depression as involving a deficiency of serotonin, and thus to think of serotonin as a mood elevating substance, but recent studies have shown that this may dramatically oversimplify the way these drugs work. "Some people will actually come to me and say, 'My serotonin must be low,'" said Dr. Joseph Deltito, lecturer in psychopharmacology at Harvard Medical School. "In fact, it's much more complicated than that, and we're beginning to realize that psychiatry doesn't even begin to understand the process."

Recent evidence seems to suggest that where there are small amounts of serotonin present, the neurons work harder to make the most of what is there, and these smaller amounts of serotonin in effect become more potent. If the person then takes Prozac, the synaptic cleft is flushed with serotonin. But the drug takes time to have an effect; by the time the person begins to feel different, the thinking goes, the system has reacted to the increase in serotonin by becoming *less responsive* to it. The mood-elevating effect appears to be related to this lowering of sensitivity to the neurotransmitter, rather than to the actual presence of the neurotransmitter.

All of this is by way of noting how complicated the work of neurotransmitters is, and therefore how tentative is any attempt to draw conclusions about the biochemistry of religious experience. And serotonin is just one neurotransmitter. In fact, the family to which serotonin and dopamine belong is responsible for only a tiny percentage of the neurotransmitter activity in the brain. "The point is that psychopharmacology is an empirical science," said Deltito. "We do something and then wait to see what happens. It's a series of black box experiments: you give input *a* and get output *b*, but we're not really sure what's happening inside."

Risperdal, as an antipsychotic, blocks certain dopamine receptors. Dopamine has been called the chief substance in the brain's "reward system." In addition to fueling the high of psychosis, it is also the part of the brain that stimulants such as cocaine and amphetamines affect: like antipsychotics, cocaine blocks dopamine receptors; amphetamines actually stimulate the production of dopamine. In fact, an overdose of amphetamines can lead to a psychotic episode.

An educated guess as to the biochemistry of psychotic experience (and perhaps of mystical experience) is that it is due, at least in part, to an excess of dopamine. Risperdal and most other antipsychotic drugs block the dopamine receptors in neurons, thus presumably thwarting the system's ability to process the excess. Result: the voices stop, the visions vanish, the basis for the delusional worldview one has created shrivels. Why this particular antipsychotic quelled Margaret's Satan delusion when others had not is anybody's guess. Risperdal differs from most earlier antipsychotics, however, in that in addition to blocking a particular dopamine receptor, it also blocks one of the serotonin receptors; studies have shown that it is more effective than earlier antipsychotics at reducing or eliminating a combination of so-called positive symptoms of psychotic illness (hallucinations, visions, exaggerated behavior) and negative symptoms (listlessness, apathy, inattention). Presumably the specific combination of serotonin and dopamine receptor sites that Risperdal affects hit Margaret right where her demon lived. It is worth noting, however, that the drug did not have the effect of "turning off" a religious preoccupation.

Margaret today is as intensely focused on spiritual issues as she ever was; rather, the drug altered her spiritual polarity, much as Buber argued a spiritually attuned psychotherapy could do when he talked about helping a patient to strengthen the "positive pole." (It should be noted that studies have demonstrated that psychotherapy also brings about chemical changes in the brain.)

In trying to connect spirituality and brain chemistry, then, one might reason thusly: *if* mysticism and at least some forms of psychosis are biochemically identical experiences (and are only distinguished by secondary factors, such as how they are perceived by society and/or the individual's personality structure); and *if* the neurotransmitter dopamine is the operative chemical in psychosis ("the dopamine hypothesis of schizophrenia" is the current reigning explanation for that disease), then dopamine may be the God chemical, the heavenly substance that breaks down the I-It walls and allows for the way of knowing that we call mystical.

However, the situation, even as it is currently understood, is vastly more complicated. For one thing, serotonin may also play an important role in religious experience, as Margaret's case may suggest. A 1995 study of neurotransmitter activity found that ritual religious fasting, which naturally tends to occur during periods of prayer and other heightened spiritual activity, enhances the transmission of serotonin between neurons, and thus may help to induce a spiritual state.[9] Serotonin, therefore, may turn out to be as much of a spiritual neurotransmitter as dopamine.

By this time one may begin to wonder how much sense it makes to try to isolate a particular chunk or process of the brain as responsible for religious experience. That may turn out to be like expecting one part of the body to be chiefly responsible for the ability to play baseball. It may be that the whole organism operates in concert, with one or another region taking brief solos while the ensemble keeps playing, so that trying to isolate particular notes or instruments becomes a purely academic exercise.

Granted that possibility, and the still infantile state of research into the biology of spirituality, we might still want to claim that these studies provide some evidence for a physical mechanism at work in the brain that may bring about spiritual states of consciousness. A select group of neurotransmitters, let us say, potentially could be the "pineal gland," the place where physiology and spirituality merge.

But if we made that claim would we be in danger of short-changing reality because of our own narrow-mindedness? As Joseph Deltito said, brain chemistry studies are all black box experiments: we don't really know what's going on inside. Even a very sophisticated and compelling biochemical understanding of what takes place during a spiritual experience does not necessarily provide an *explanation* of the experience. According to one view, there are many phenomena for which science as we now understand it does not have answers, even partial answers. The feisty intercessory prayer movement, whose proponents include scientists and religious professionals and whose chief spokesman is former National Institutes of Health physician Larry Dossey, promotes research that purports to show that praying for the recovery of patients, who do not know they are being prayed for, who may live in another city from those doing the praying, and who do not even know the people doing the praying, results in those patients recovering faster and more fully than control groups who were not prayed for. Other intercessory prayer studies have focused on praying for the health of animals, bacteria, and fungi, all of which supposedly benefited from the prayers. (Certainly in the latter instances psychological factors can't be involved—no one can claim that a fungus is swayed to health by the thought that someone might be praying for it.)

Such studies purportedly demonstrate a kind of communication that is not explainable by biology and physics as they are commonly understood. If a sick woman knows she is being prayed for and becomes well, one might suppose that that knowledge produced changes in her brain chemistry, which in turn affected her body. Her belief that prayer works would, in effect, make the prayer work. This is one explanation for the placebo effect. The intercessory prayer studies, however, take away that explanation, and leave us with no substitute mechanism to explain the results. If these studies were confirmed and amplified, the case would be made for a far broader, wilder way of looking at spirituality and psychology: the psyche-spirit movement as it is outlined in this book might be only stage one of some sort of unified field theory that brought together physics, psychology, and spirituality and transcended all of those areas as they are now understood. We would be in true *X-Files* territory.

According to Marilyn Schlitz, director of research at the Institute of Noetic Sciences, studies on intercessory prayer show the reality of "non-local informational or energetic exchange between two people or between two biological systems," and they point to the need for "an expanded epistemology of science."[10]

People who are reluctant to give credence to such studies as these often do not have a hard time accepting some of the seemingly antiscientific postulations of particle physics, such as "action at a distance," according to which subatomic particles at opposite ends of the universe can communicate instantaneously with one another. If we took either of these noncommonsensical postulates as a caution that the universe of all that we do not understand is very wide indeed, we might want to hedge our bets about the interaction of body and soul. We might say that evidence suggests not that there is necessarily a neurological *basis* for religious experience, but that there are biochemical factors associated with it. If that was as far as we were willing to go, the psyche-spirit movement would have something like the following as an underlying claim:

• There is reason to suspect that some psychotic experiences and some religious experiences are identical. This area of overlap involves the feeling of the dissolution of the boundaries between self and other.

• This overlap suggests a biochemical factor in religious experience. However, it may be premature to conclude that the biochemical factors are the real underlying explanation of the experiences.

• Spirituality, then, has a real biological component but should not be reduced to mere biology. It, like psychosis, may be far stranger than our current imaginings allow. In other words, we may be wise to reserve for religious experience the dignity of mystery—we may not want to reduce it to the level of brain chemistry.

But in maintaining this reserve, are we avoiding what seems the most likely explanation because it makes us uncomfortable? One difficulty with this limited conclusion is that we are conditioned to accept—to insist—that mental illness is biologically determined. Indeed, many mental patients find comfort in this—an absolution from guilt—which counseling centers encourage, as in an advertisement for one that read: "Depression is a flaw in chemistry not character. For free information call. . . ." If we grant that psychosis can be accounted for by brain chemistry, and if we are willing to associate some forms of psychosis with some forms of religious experience, then shouldn't we be ready to acknowledge that religion—at least in its most intense, crystallized form, the mystical experience—really does happen due to certain explosions or secretions in the brain?

It is possible to push further for an answer to this question. Most scientific investigations of religious experience have involved mere observation of the experience. What if it were possible to set up a study in which one activated a religious experience by chemical means? That might give us further encouragement to find one foundation for all experience and all reality—material, spiritual, psychological. It would ground the psyche-spirit movement in a deep and fascinating way, providing the basis for further exploration of the science of spirituality. It would vindicate William James. And it would make it much more difficult to separate the domains of psychiatrists and clergy.

11

Acid Flashback

In his trial-and-error life explorations man almost everywhere has stumbled upon connections between vegetables (eaten or brewed) and actions (yogic breathing exercises, whirling dervish dances, flagellations) which altered states of consciousness. From the psychopharmacological standpoint we now understand these states to be the products of changes in brain chemistry. From the sociological perspective we see that they tended to be connected in some way with religion.

—Huston Smith

To me it's always been a proof of God.

—Ken Kesey

One of the ten primordial elements that Paul Fleischman identifies in his work exploring the intersection of psychiatry and religion—basic human needs that both religion and psychiatry serve—is release. Transcendence is a goal of all religions. Where once psychology focused on the need to strengthen the self, now the emphasis is more often on loosening it up. We all know that we need to let go, to get away. We take vacations, watch television, jump out of airplanes, dive to the sea bottom, take up watercolors, roam the Internet, drink, surf, climb, sail, paint, putt, putter—it's all part of the same lifelong attempt to escape. But from what? From the crusty collection of habits, tics, and behaviors that together form the self, which is for each of us the center of everything and also a choking, ossifying tomb. Some of the avenues we take to escape from it, paradoxically, strengthen those habits and tics at the same time (if you're lazy you escape by watching TV), but still the motivation is to *let go*.

The mystery inherent in letting go—the reason we value it and crave it—may have to do with the idea that in abandoning the self we are, somehow or other, moving closer to the self. We are embracing the wider self, which we spend so much of our time holding at bay.

There are, arguably, two preeminent forms of release, two that surpass all others in how far and how truly they fling us from our center. Religion is the socially sanctioned one, and drugs are its dark twin. Society hates drugs not because, as hype would have it, drugs take you nowhere, but because they take you somewhere—to a place where, it is feared, the terrain will be unfamiliar, where you might get lost and never come home, and also where the wanton side of you, the side that detests the tomb of the self, may want to stay permanently.

Of course, we do not think of these two experiences as closely related; we dare not, for indeed drugs *are* dangerous, and the danger comes from the push-button ease with which their journey is enacted.

Most things that can be said of drugs can also be said of mysticism. It too is a solo pursuit. It too is a high. Religions have been built up around it in order to harness it, to make the ecstatic flash that comes with breaking through the I-it boundary useful, but as religions become institutions they inevitably come to downplay and belittle and mock the mystical experience. It is, after all, so very different from them. They are of the social fabric: rational, sober, with duties that extend from guiding the upbringing of children to ensuring that dead bodies are thoughtfully disposed of. Religion is heavy with responsibility. Mysticism is none of those things: it is a long, sweet ride on the wave, with such focus and blissful intensity that the rider and the wave merge. It has often been said that mystics of all traditions—Sufi, Christian, Kabbalistic, Hindu—have more in common with one another than any of them do with the religions in which each resides. The similarity of reported mystical experiences around the world and through time was one body of evidence that led William James to conclude that spirituality is basically one thing: that the plurality of the world's religions are only different manifestations of the same religion, different staircases, variously carved and polished, that all lead to the same place. Religions are many—mysticism is one.

The parallels between mysticism and drugs are so close it is not surprising that some people have long believed mystical experience and certain drug experiences to be identical. Indeed, if religion and mysticism were once closely joined, so too religion and certain drugs were once linked. And, far from being a device of countercultural expression, these drugs—that is to say, naturally occurring psychoactive substances—were part of the cultural cement of ancient societies; their use was regulated by the establishment for the furtherance of its aims. The earliest evidence for the ritual use of psychoactive drugs dates to 800 B.C. Soma, the elixir of the gods used in the Vedic sacrifices in ancient India, was derived from a hallucinogenic plant, possibly the mushroom *Amanita muscaria*. Haoma, a ritual substance similarly used in Iran at least as far back as the fifth century B.C., may have been made from the same mushroom. Some people have suggested that religion itself came into being only after the path to spiritual experience was opened by ingesting or smoking some mind-altering plant.

The ancient Greeks gave the world the science of reason, true rational philosophy, a way to separate ourselves from nature and so began to order it, analyze it, and tame it. But for two thousand years—from pre-Homeric times until Christianizing invasions in the fourth century—the ancient Greeks also took part in the ritual known as the Eleusinian mysteries, a ceremonial celebration of the myth of Demeter and Persephone, of the changing seasons and the autumnal "death" of nature, the highlight of which was an ecstatic merging of the individual with nature. This experience was generally held to be the most profound and enlightening moment of a person's life. The ritual involved fasting, a procession from Athens to the sanctuary at Eleusis, singing and chanting, and, at its height, the drinking of an apparently mind-altering substance called kykeon. According to one theory this herbal brew was probably made from ergot, a fungus that grows on wild cereal and grass plants, which has strong psychoactive properties. The civilization that was the birthplace of rationalism considered a nonrational union of the individual with the universe, probably aided by a drug, to be its most sacred experience.

A scientific search for religious experience that involves studying neurotransmitters or scanning the brains of meditating monks can't prove, even by its own criteria, that whatever biochemical mechanism it isolates as involved in the experience is responsible for the experience. That is because such studies are merely passive observations of a process; what they observe may or may not be operative. But when someone drops a hit of LSD or imbibes a sacred mushroom potion that person is activating a process: if you take LSD and see God, there is no escaping the conclusion that the drug and the heavenly experience are causally related. So here at least, we can forget about intercessory prayer and action at a distance: here we are in the zone of relatively familiar science. *This* chemical caused *that* feeling or state. If, therefore, we could equate that state with religious states in general—if we could find a way to show that the acid heaven and the church heaven were the same place— we might consider it a crucial piece of evidence to support other studies that show a biological basis for religious experience: we might be able to say that we have found an actual, honest-to-God scientific grounding for the psyche-spirit movement, for an expanded view of human beings that includes technologically sophisticated, no-nonsense medicine, the lush intricacies of psychotherapy, and spiritual longing and release. Or, to put it in philosophical terminology, if we have ruled out Cartesian dualism—the theory that reality is composed of two substances, matter and mind/soul—then the remaining possibilities are that All is Matter or All is Mind; if we could convince ourselves that chemicals bring about mystical states, that would tilt us toward one of those two options.

The fact that important past civilizations, upon which ours rests in so many other ways, linked psychoactive substances and religion provides one argument in support of that claim. Added to that, there are still cultures that preach psychedelic transcendence. Eleusis fell to ruins a long time ago, but the experience is not so far removed from us. In churches and homes scattered across the Midwest and Southwest of the United States, members of the Native American Church to this day use peyote as a religious sacrament. Peyote (from the Aztec for "divine messenger"), which comes from a cactus and contains the drug mescaline, has evidently been part of religious ritual in Central America for millennia. Its use spread to North American Indians in the late nineteenth and early twentieth centuries; as Indians were being subdued and forced onto reservations, they blended the peyote rite with Christian beliefs and with various beliefs inherited from their forebears. Roughly 250,000 people in the United States practice this faith. Their right to eat peyote buttons and drink peyote tea as part of their service, and so enter a state of immediate experience of universal oneness, was acknowledged by the U.S. government with the passing of a federal law in 1994. In 1997, Native Americans in the armed forces won the right to use peyote for religious purposes while in service.

Of course, the point is not that religious experience must or ought to come through chemicals, but that it may. Testing this theory would require an experiment, and just such an experiment was once conducted. Mike Young, a sixty-year-old minister in Honolulu, participated in it. He is someone who knows the Eleusinian mystery—or something like it—firsthand. On Good Friday in 1962, while a graduate student at Andover Theological Seminary in Boston, Young took part in a kind of modern reenactment of Eleusis, a ceremony that was at once scientific experiment and religio-pharmacological exercise. It changed his life: "It made me look at who I am, how I am, what I might become—it changed my idea of what a religious experience is, and made me surer about becoming a minister." It was also a defining moment in the formation of the cultural myth surrounding the decade of the 1960s. It has gone down in cultural lore as the Marsh Chapel Experiment, or the Good Friday Experiment.

To put it in context requires backing up in time—to 1943. On a sunny afternoon in April of that year, with war raging throughout Europe, Dr. Albert Hofmann, a Swiss chemist, mounted his bicycle and began pedaling through the glorious Swiss countryside from his laboratory to his home. The play of sunlight and the imminent arrival of spring were, however, lost on him. Over the past several years he had been studying the chemical properties of the fungus ergot, with the idea of eventually isolating a drug that the chemical company he worked for could market. From ancient times through the Middle Ages ergot was renowned for a number of different properties: it was a poison that had been responsible for many mass epidemics when it had contaminated bread, but it was also used during pregnancy to induce labor. Hofmann had had the idea to isolate the chemical derivatives of its active substance and try to find one that might be marketed for obstetric use. Three days earlier, while working with the twenty-fifth isolate he had produced of the active substance, lysergic acid or LSD-25, he had gotten some of it on his hands and found himself plunged into "a dreamlike state" in which he perceived "an uninterrupted stream of fantastic pictures, extraordinary shapes with intense, kaleidoscopic play of colors." He decided to make a proper self-experimentation of the drug, and so, accompanied by an assistant, administered to himself the smallest dose he could imagine would have any effect.

The LSD was beginning to take hold as he began his bicycle journey (to this day the psychedelic community celebrates April 19 as "Bicycle Day," the date of the first acid trip): "Everything in my field of vision wavered and was distorted as if seen in a curved mirror." Shortly after arriving at his home he became convinced that "a demon had invaded me, had taken possession of my body, mind and soul." His doctor and his wife were at his side, but they could do nothing but watch as he went through all the phases of a massive LSD trip. By morning, out in his garden with the sun shining after a light rain, he experienced the world "as if newly created." Most impressive to Hofmann was the seeming contradiction that while his consciousness stayed intact throughout the experience, so that he could later recall and record it in precise detail, the altered state of consciousness also involved the dissolution of the boundary between himself and the world: he was not "capable, by any act of will, of preventing the breakdown of the world around me."[1] The drug had somehow given him the experience of release of "self" while preserving, in some corner of his mind, self-consciousness.*

In the 1940s and 1950s, LSD was a mystery, both scientifically and phenomenologically. It was a source of fascination—not yet a cultural bogeyman. First in Switzerland, and then elsewhere in Europe and the United States, LSD studies were undertaken on animals and humans. (The animal tests were found to be nearly useless, because, as was soon discovered, the experience was essentially subjective and required the subject to report on what he or she had experienced.) From the 1920s research had also been conducted on the psychoactive effects of mescaline and other naturally occurring chemicals. LSD differed most notably from all of these in the intensity of its effects and in potency: LSD is somewhere between five thousand and ten thousand times more potent than mescaline. But it was also qualitatively different, affecting, in the words of Hofmann, who went on to conduct hallucinogen experiments for the next two decades, "the highest control centers of the psychic and intellectual functions."

Indeed, the earliest tests of LSD on humans showed how little researchers understood about the effect of the drug. In the early 1950s a major LSD research project took place at Spring Grove State Hospital in Maryland, in which LSD was given to schizophrenics. The patients received daily doses of the drug, beginning with 100 micrograms and increasing by 100 micrograms every day for five days. In comparison, the

---

*The same phenomenon—loss of self with preservation of self-consciousness or awareness—was noted by Robert Forman, professor of religion at Hunter College, in a study of the reported mystical experiences of religious figures throughout history, which Forman presented at the 1996 "Toward a Science of Consciousness" symposium. Forman identifies a type of mystical state he calls a "pure consciousness event," which he defines as "a wakeful but non-intentional (objectless) consciousness." In this state, he says, "one's consciousness persists even though all mental content is suspended." Forman concludes that this is evidence that consciousness is broader than our everyday experience suggests.

average hit of blotter acid in the 1960s contained 100 to 300 micrograms of LSD; in other words, these mental patients were given enough of the drug to launch a full-blown trip every day for five straight days. And yet, as the researchers found, the results were highly variable. As one later review of the experiment put it: "The basic assumptions that indirectly guided this research included the conjecture that LSD could be given on a daily basis to patients in order to produce a chemotherapeutic effect as with other psychiatric drugs. It was assumed that the effects of LSD could be adequately observed and understood by trained clinicians not directly involved with the patient's treatment, who had no prior relationship with the patient."[2] In fact, the researchers soon realized they were dealing with a substance that did not work with anything like the straightforwardness of other drugs. One woman who was given LSD in the Spring Grove experiment, who had been catatonic and mute for several years, suddenly commenced laughing, crying, chatting, giggling, playing basketball, and smiling. That evening, she attended a dance at the hospital and danced with a fellow patient. The next morning, she was catatonic again. Two more daily injections, with increased dosages, did nothing to waken her from her stupor. "Observations like these," the report concluded, "helped the team to realize that this drug was unlike other psychoactive medications because of its unique combination of dramatic alterations in consciousness, profound psychodynamic action as well as the rapid building of tolerance."[3] Put another way, researchers were beginning to realize that the effects of this substance, since it operated on the central nervous system, were unusually dependent on the subject's state of mind, the setting, and other psychological factors.

One thing scientists noted during these early experiments was that the drug often caused subjects to relive long-buried experiences; this led to a long series of studies exploring the possibilities of "LSD-assisted psychotherapy," in which the drug's mind-expanding properties would help to open blocked areas of personality. By one estimate, from the 1940s to the 1960s LSD studies resulted in more than one thousand scientific papers and included forty thousand patients. During this heyday of psychedelic research hundreds of laboratory scientists made the decision to devote themselves to what they saw as a highly promising field. A body of data was compiled that seemed to indicate that psychoactive substances had remarkable effects in areas as diverse as chronic pain relief, depression, and drug addiction.

Stanislav Grof, the Czech-born psychiatrist who, with Abraham Maslow, helped found the field of transpersonal psychology, became a leader of the LSD-assisted psychotherapy movement. Grof's extensive research, involving hundreds of patients, led him to conclude that psychoactive compounds work on memory (allowing subjects to relive past events) and also push the mind beyond the space-time boundaries of ordinary consciousness into a realm that could be called mystical or transpersonal. After drug experimentation was halted by the government in the early 1970s, Grof developed a technique he called holotropic breathwork, basically a controlled form of hyperventilation, as a way to break through to nonordinary states of consciousness. This technique, which Grof modeled on the breathing rituals of Eastern religions, is still taught today.

While clinical LSD research was continuing, freelance explorations with LSD, mescaline, and psilocybin were becoming more common, with people meeting in groups to explore what many believed were spiritual pathways that the drugs opened. In 1954 Aldous Huxley published *The Doors of Perception*, based on his experiences with mescaline and in which he laid out the argument that such chemicals opened channels of experience that ordinary consciousness kept closed, and thus gave a wider view of reality, one that was virtually identical to mystical experience.

All of this went on in an atmosphere of innocence that seems hard to believe today. LSD was legal, and the Sandoz laboratory in Switzerland, for which Hofmann had worked while discovering the chemical and which owned the patent on LSD-25, routinely filled orders for the drug and mailed them to whoever paid the modest fee. The prevalence of LSD stirred scientific interest in other hallucinogens. Over six weeks in 1961, researchers from Harvard University gave psilocybin to thirty-five prisoner-volunteers from the maximum-security Massachusetts Correctional Institute. The idea was to test whether the drug had any effect on rates of recidivism. Six months after their release, only 25 percent of the "hallucinogenic prisoners" had been re-arrested—an impressive statistic when compared with the average of 64 percent for the prison population as a whole. But what surprised the researchers was that during and after the drug experiences the prisoners—few of whom had had more than a high school education—talked of the experience in terms reminiscent of the great mystics of world religious history.

One Harvard clinician involved in the study, Timothy Leary, was especially impressed by this seeming spiritual effect of the chemical. Leary was not yet the Mad Hatter of LSD, but a rather brilliant young psychologist with an expertise in personality testing. What, he wondered, would happen if the drug were given in something like the way it was administered in ancient cultures, as part of an actual religious service? All of the studies of psychedelic drugs done up to that time had taken place in clinical settings, in sterile rooms, with lab-coated scientists peering down at the subjects, peppering them with questions: hardly an atmosphere conducive to fostering mystical union. The following year Leary and his Harvard colleague Richard Alpert (who would later rename himself Ram Dass) served as faculty advisors for Dr. Walter Pahnke, a psychiatrist who was in the process of obtaining his Ph.D. from Harvard Divinity School, in an unprecedented experiment Pahnke had devised as part of his dissertation research. They gathered twenty seminary students and explained that they wanted their help to explore the psychobiology of religious experience. They prepared the students by conducting physical and psychological examinations on each, then brought them to a small chapel on the campus of Boston University. The experiment was double-blind: ten students were given psilocybin, the other ten were given dummy pills; no one knew which students were given which. The students then took part in a two-and-a-half-hour Christian worship service, with organ music, prayer readings, and sonorous oratory from the Rev. Howard Thurman, chaplain of Boston University. The idea, according to Pahnke, was to create "an atmosphere broadly comparable to that achieved by tribes who actually use natural psychedelic substances in religious ceremonies."[4] They chose Good Friday, which Christians celebrate as the anniversary of Christ's death on the cross, as a time when the religious feelings of seminarians would likely be heightened. It was also, coincidentally or not, the closest Christian parallel to the Eleusinian celebration of the return of Persephone to Hades, the death of nature and the onset of winter. Like the Greek mystery rite, Good Friday ritualized religion's darkest hour—the death of God.

Mike Young was one of those who got the real drug. Thirty-five years later, the experience was still vivid. As the worship service progressed and he and his colleagues sat or knelt in pews, he recalled, colors began to burn like flames, movements caused trails of light, objects became outlined with geometric imagery. The students began to realize who had and had not gotten the drug, as some pointed out depths of wonder in the flickering flames of the candles that others didn't see.

Thurman's sermon was, naturally, about death, tragedy, and the mystery of rebirth; it fairly glowed with dark light. As it progressed, those who had taken the drug felt pulled into the blackness at the bottom of life. One began writhing on the floor, hearing the voice of his uncle, a minister who had recently died, say to him, "I want you to die," over and over. "The more that I let go and sort of died," the subject said much later in trying to describe the mystical nature of the experience, "the more I felt this eternal life . . . just in that one session I think I gained experience I didn't have before and probably could never have gotten from a hundred hours of reading or a thousand hours of reading."[5]

At the center of the service and the trip, Mike Young could no longer distinguish what was going on inside his mind from what was taking place in the outside world. A vision of a mandala rose up around him. It raged with color, and each of its spiraling bands was "a different life experience." He was in the center; he realized that he had to follow one of these paths, or die. But he couldn't choose. He sat frozen in horror. And then, he said, "I died." He was bathed, engulfed by, drowning in the experience of Christ's death. It was his own personal Good Friday.

Years later, he recalled the moment and saw that he had in fact made a choice: to let his old self die, so that a new one would come into being. As a middle-aged man, Young realized that the experience had been inextricably psychological and spiritual. The mandala image had represented the psychological struggle of a young man wrestling with the question of what to do with his life. The religious nature of the experience only dawned on him over time: "I was raised as a Baptist, and I had a Sunday School idea of what a religious experience was: something hoary and angelic. This was agony, a total transformation, which was terribly painful. It took time for me to equate that with religion, with the long dark night of the soul, to realize the difference between an intellectual understanding of what religion is and actually experiencing it."

Pahnke gave his subjects two questionnaires, one immediately after the experience and one six months later. The questions were based on a "typology of the mystical state of consciousness" he had drawn from various published analyses of mystical experience, including William James's criteria and, especially, that detailed by the philosopher W. T. Stace in his 1960 book *Mysticism and Philosophy*. Pahnke identified nine features of the state, including individual unity with outer reality, transcendence of time and space, and profound positive feelings. The test group ranked high in nearly every category, while the control group scored low in every category. For example, when asked a series of questions regarding whether the service had engendered in them a feeling that they had transcended the bounds of time and space, 84 percent of the answers of those who had taken the drug were affirmative, and only 6 percent of those of the control group were.

The point of the experiment was not simply to ascertain whether psilocybin had any effect over and against a control group, but whether, when taken in a religious setting, its effects approximated those of previously identified mystical states. It was, and still remains, the most thorough and exacting scientific study ever undertaken on the question of whether the "escape" of psychoactive drugs and the transcendence of religious experience are the same thing.* Both the data and

---

*The study did have some flaws, however, chiefly Pahnke's downplaying of or failure to record many of the subjects' negative reactions to the drug: the life-and-death psycho-spiritual struggles they endured during the experience. Most egregiously, Pahnke failed to indicate in his write-up of the experiment that one subject had to be tranquilized by an injection of thorazine. In most other ways, however, Pahnke followed rigorous experimentation procedures, and the detailed questionnaire he devised to analyze the mystical nature of the experience formed the basis for later social scientific studies of mystical experience.

Pahnke's own impressions from interviewing the subjects suggested that they were: Pahnke wrote that he was "left with the impression that the experience had made a profound impact (especially in terms of religious feeling and thinking) on the lives of eight out of ten of the subjects who had been given psilocybin."

Pahnke optimistically concluded that his research might form the basis for further study of the psychobiology of religious experience. He imagined that psychology would thereafter move in the direction William James had envisioned and begin full-scale studies of the mechanisms by which psychoactive substances work and to what extent they lead to religious awakening. (James had also explored the possibility of using substances to short-circuit the path to transcendence. He himself used nitrous oxide and found that it and ether "stimulate the mystical consciousness in an extraordinary degree. . . . Looking back on my own experiences, they all converge toward a kind of insight to which I cannot help ascribing some metaphysical significance." Whereas James freely admitted to a lack of a natural mystical awareness of transcendent truth, he also insisted that such an awareness did come to him in "the artificial mystic state of mind.")[6]

What Pahnke envisioned was not to be. Within a few years, LSD and other drugs were widely adopted for recreational use, Timothy Leary went off the edge, Charles Manson became the worst possible poster boy for LSD, bad trips were taken—in short, the sixties happened, and what once seemed innocently interesting turned ominous and ugly. The Food and Drug Administration slammed the door on virtually all scientific testing of the effects of hallucinogens. Walter Pahnke's Marsh Chapel Experiment—about which Walter Houston Clark, the respected psychologist of religion and winner of the American Psychological Association's William James Memorial Award, wrote, "There are no experiments known to me in the history of the scientific study of religion better designed or clearer in their conclusions," and which, in 1966 *Time* reported on in grandiose terms, declaring it a milestone and proclaiming that all of those who had taken the drug had achieved "a mystical consciousness that resembled those described by saints and ascetics"— became not a new path to a future psychology of religion but, due to the publicity it got, a catalyst for the 1960s freelance drug culture.

Pahnke had intended to do a twenty-five-year follow-up to the study, to assess whether the experience had had any lasting affect, but he died in 1971. In the late 1980s, Rick Doblin, himself a Harvard graduate student, decided, as part of his own research, to do the follow-up. He tracked down most of the participants, interviewed them, and readministered the questionnaire. The results were even more impressive than before: the psilocybin respondents actually ranked the experience higher in most of Pahnke's categories of mystical experience than they had twenty-five years earlier. Where Pahnke had found eight of the ten who had received the drug believed the experience had a religious impact on them, Doblin found that all ten now believed so: "Each of the psilocybin subjects felt that the experience had significantly affected his life in a positive way and expressed appreciation for having participated in the experiment." What's more, Doblin found that several of these people had gone on to careers that involved them in social or political activism, and they linked that involvement to their Good Friday experience, which gave them a lasting feeling of unity with others.[7]

From about 1970, the lack of interest in exploring how certain drugs interact with brain chemistry and what that might tell us about the nature of religious experience was near absolute. Then, as the 1990s dawned, paralleling the renewal of interest in the Jamesian vision in psychology was a return of interest in psychedelics. Just as the psyche-spirit movement of the 1990s has been a more measured and institutionalized version of what were mostly free-form longings in the 1960s, the new focus on psychedelics is also deliberate, clinical, "sober." As with the psyche-spirit movement, many of the scientists leading laboratory investigations of psychedelic substances today got their first experience of the substances as students in the 1960s.

Most of the studies that have received FDA approval have more obvious and straightforward potential benefits than Pahnke's work did, but all seek to exploit the way these drugs interact with brain chemistry in order to ameliorate suffering that might be thought of as psychospiritual in nature. Beginning in 1993, studies got under way examining how MDMA ("ecstasy"), psilocybin, and ibogaine (a drug derived from the iboga plant, whose leaves are used in rites of passage ceremonies in West Africa), might be used in, respectively, the treatment of chronic pain in cancer patients, psychotherapy, and treatment of cocaine addiction.

But to many in the field, the moment of truth would come when LSD itself reentered the lab. Ironically, the psychedelic compound most synonymous with abuse had shown the greatest medical potential. In 1998, Richard Yensen, a psychologist in Baltimore, was nearing final government approval of an elaborate proposal to study "LSD-assisted psychotherapy" as a treatment for alcohol addiction. When and if his work gets under way, researchers in the fledgling psychedelics field believe it will signal that a psychological barrier that has been in place for three decades will have been broken down.

The idea of psychedelics as a cure for addiction may seem oxymoronic, or at least very strange, but to Yensen it has been a lifelong crusade. He was one of those young scientists in the

1960s who decided to dedicate their work to psychedelics but were thwarted by the forces of history. In the early 1970s he became a research fellow at the Maryland Psychiatric Research Center, which, several years earlier, under the directorship of Stanislav Grof and with the backing of Governor Spiro Agnew (of all people), became the nation's premier psychedelic research institute. Yensen thus caught the tail end of the era of clinical experimentation with psychedelic drugs, and saw enough to convince him that this was his life's work: "I was a young man, I'd just got my Ph.D., and I anticipated becoming a tenured researcher. I watched LSD change damaged personalities. I watched dying patients suddenly find meaning in their lives and become close with their families in their last days. I watched alcoholics give up their addiction and put their lives together."

Yensen also watched as Timothy Leary, whom he had admired in the early days, steered the psychedelic ship in another direction. "Tim Leary was a friend," he said, "but there came a time when I could no longer call him a colleague. He became morally reprehensible. He set us back decades."

Yensen decided that he would ride out the hard times. It turned out to be a long ride. After teaching at Harvard Medical School and Johns Hopkins University, he teamed up with his wife, psychiatrist Donna Dryer, to found a psychotherapy institute in Baltimore that they hoped would become the center for new LSD work. They then spent ten years lobbying the FDA, the DEA, and the state legislature. They have screened their first subjects: alcoholics who live in the Baltimore area and who have a "significant other" willing to assist in the grueling process in which subjects, under the influence, dredge up repressed memories, battle with long-buried foes, and try to overcome the psychological forces that drove them to drink in the first place. They have a team in place ready to provide 120 hours of psychotherapy and one to five LSD experiences for each patient. Yensen hopes to show that because of the still mysterious process by which LSD works the patients "will be motivated to decrease their abuse of substances and lead more satisfactory lives." A second proposed study would test LSD with the terminally ill.

But how is it possible that psychedelic drugs could have potential to heal in so many seemingly disparate areas? The answer seems to be twofold: the areas—terminal illness, drug addiction, alcoholism, and depression treatment for the elderly—are not so disparate; and the compounds being brought to bear on them are not like other drugs. " 'Drugs' is probably not the best word to describe these substances," Yensen said. "The things we call drugs are substances like aspirin, which has its analgesic property whether you take it with somebody you love or somebody you hate and despite whatever you may think about the person who gave it to you. The operation of the psychedelics is biochemical, but they do not have a drug property. They operate on the complex processes going on in our central nervous system—in other words, on the system by which all of our experience is understood and processed."

A 1996 study of psilocybin shed some light on these neuropsychological workings of psychoactive substances. Test subjects and a control group were asked to play a word recognition game in which a series of letters is flashed and one has to identify when they are random characters and when there is a word present. Earlier studies showed that people can locate a word more quickly if its set of characters is preceded by one in which a related word figures: if "snow" is in the first set, a normal person will more quickly spot "ice" in the next. But this rapid recognition, which psychologists call semantic priming, only works for closely related words, and not for indirectly related words, such as "lemon" and "sweet." However, the subjects under the influence of psilocybin were able to take advantage of semantic priming with indirectly related words and so identify the second word faster. Schizophrenics also have this ability, although both in the case of schizophrenics and psilocybin subjects it comes at a price: ordinary semantic priming with closely related words suffers. The study provides a tentative way of objectifying the subjective nature of the experience by showing how the drug (and the schizophrenia) can lead to what the researchers concluded was a kind of broadened consciousness and expanded creativity (although at the expense of normal logic).[8]

"Psychedelics introduce a certain chaos or noise into the central nervous system" is how Yensen explains this effect. "Out of that chaos come possible insights about the origin of problems, the nature of life, the sense of encountering an ultimate reality that is deeper than the one we live in every day. This is how these substances can lead to a peak experience, which allows someone to reorient his or her life around a central, positive core. But none of these experiences are in the drug. Having a peak experience, for example, depends on a complex set of factors: a good relationship with the person you are having the experience with, a proper environment, music, maybe having pictures of your family around you. These substances have been valued throughout human history, they've been called sacred for most of the cultures that have used them. I think the people of those cultures were alluding to a unique property, where it is possible to touch the highest levels of humanity through the aegis of these substances, when used in the right way."

As far as Yensen is concerned, there is little difference between the overtly religious use to which these substances have been put in various cultures and the more clinical guise in which they are appearing in research projects today. "Glimpsing heaven" is not academically respectable, but relieving pain, which may be a manifestation of end-of-life anguish, is, and breaking the cycle of addiction is.

Mike Young spots an irony in this recent turn of events. In 1995 he became pastor of a new church in Honolulu, and he wanted both to "confess" his participation in the Marsh Chapel experiment to his new congregation and also to talk to them about what he saw as the psychospiritual potential of psychoactive drugs. In a sermon on the subject, he outlined some of the new research under way, and then concluded, "What a wonderful irony to all of this: at the moment it is completely illegal for a religious leader to administer a religious experience to you in this way. But it is quite legal for a scientist to administer a religious experience to you in this way. The irony . . . is that we have indeed made the scientists the high priests of our technological society. Those same high priests are now finding that they are in fact going to have to learn how to be priests for real."[9]

Young is ahead of the curve—few people are as willing to equate psychedelic and religious experiences. But if he, Richard Yensen, and others who are involved in the movement to renew full-scale laboratory testing of these substances are right, then this work may go far toward establishing a scientific grounding for an expanded view of the self or psyche—one that includes the soul, one that embraces William James's belief that "the conscious person is continuous with a wider self."

Huston Smith, the grand old man of comparative religion, who has held professorships at MIT and the University of California at Berkeley, has long been been of the opinion that psychoactive substances "have light to throw on the history of religion, the phenomenology of religion, the philosophy of religion, and the practice of the religious life itself." Here is how

Smith once suggested that psychedelic drugs breach the supposed physical barrier between "self " and "world":

> [W]e know that the human organism is interlaced with its world in innumerable ways it normally cannot sense—through gravitational fields, body respiration, and the like; the list could be multiplied until man's skin began to seem more like a thoroughfare than a boundary. Perhaps the deeper regions of the brain which evolved earlier and are more like those of the lower animals . . . can sense this relatedness better than can the cerebral cortex which now dominates our awareness. If so, when the drugs rearrange the neurohumors that chemically transmit impulses across synapses between neurons, man's consciousness and his submerged, intuitive, ecological awareness might for a spell become interlaced.[10]

To bring together the arguments of the last two chapters, there is evidence that at least some kind of psychosis is the same thing as at least some kind of religious experience; there is also reason to suspect not only that the altered state of consciousness brought about by LSD and related chemicals overlaps with religious or mystical states of consciousness but that the chemicals can actually bring about those mystical states.* Add to this the whole weight of contemporary psychiatry, which supposes that psychosis (and other forms of mental illness) is biochemical in origin, as well as the studies of meditat-

---

*This also implies that psychotic experience and psychoactive drug experience overlap, and indeed from the beginning of research with psychoactive drugs scientists who worked with them noted similarities between the states they produced and psychotic states. LSD in particular can produce psychotic symptoms and even a psychotic breakdown.

ing monks and other attempts to explore the biology of spirituality, and the argument begins to gather steam: religious experience does indeed have a biochemical foundation.

If we accept this, then two things follow. One is the intriguing possibility of mainstream science using psychoactive substances as shortcut passageways to religious experience for the purposes of learning more about its biological layer. When, in 1997, David Larson's National Institute for Healthcare Research conducted a broad forum on the future of scientific investigation of spirituality, its neuroscience panel—which included experts in psychiatry, pharmacology, epidemiology, and physiology from Yale, UCLA, and Duke medical schools as well as the National Institute on Drug Abuse—ranked what it called "drug-induced spiritual experiences" as among the promising areas to explore. The panel acknowledged that "for more than two decades now it has been extremely difficult to justify the actual experimental administration of these agents" but stated its belief that psychoactive compounds "can sometimes induce distinct types of mystical experiences." The panel wrote: "Exploring the effect various pharmacological agents might have on various spiritual interventions or practices might begin to delineate the role of different neurotransmitter systems in spiritual experience. . . . Neuroscientific studies of drug-induced spiritual experiences, perhaps utilizing modern imaging techniques, might help to begin to elucidate the neurobiological mechanisms involved in similar non-drug-induced spiritual experiences." Discussing LSD studies in particular, the panel said that they "offer the potential of measuring a 'dose' of a spiritual experience."[11]

The second result of accepting that religious experience has a biological foundation is philosophical or theological—the problem of Descartes's dualism is truly overcome. We are not, it seems, of two substances—matter (which is evident) and mind/soul (which *seems* evident but is in fact naggingly hard to pin down). There is only one substance, which fills the astronomical universe and the galaxies of our dreams, which comprises our bones and our gods, our lives and our deaths, our guilt and our skin and our ecstasy. It is the meat on our plates and the meat in our heads, the body of the slaughtered animal and the Body of Christ.

But in solving one problem—finding a scientific ground for the psyche-spirit movement—do we create another? If mind-body dualism is thus overcome, then the medical materialists seem to have the last laugh, for the one true and mysterious substance of reality turns out to be none other than the stuff we stub our toes on and sink our teeth into every day. The bed we have made for a new, expanded psychology to rest upon turns out to be as sharp and hard as a bed of nails. Heaven vanishes, dreams dissolve into mere static, delusions are only delusions. Spirits get punctured.

12

Experience Itself

Relation is the essence of everything that is.

—MEISTER ECKHART

Joshua Beil, whose psychotic episode informs the first chapter of this book, saw his experience as both mental illness and religious epiphany. David Lukoff confirmed that perspective for him: he gave a psychologist's stamp of authenticity to the spiritual as well as the medical reading of the episode. When in the midst of the episode Joshua observed two trees side by side and was plunged into a new state of awareness—of the "God-createdness of the tree" and "how it relates to the tree next to it" and "of the interconnectedness of matter and mind and of my place in this beautiful universe"—he was, according to this reading, literally in the place of the mystics. And when the psychosis—with its dark painful shiverings and its ecstatic flashes—vanished after a course of antipsychotic medication, it was in part due to what the last couple of chapters tried to show: that there is a biological basis not only for mental illness but for religious experience as well.

No sooner has one identified such a connection than some in the crowd perk up their ears, nod vigorously, jab their index fingers, and start their shouts of "Aha!" One feels the pull of the slippery slope of medical materialism: when the brain thinks it is communing with angels, a little voice begins to chant, it is really just high on dopamine.

The medical materialists, with whom William James jousted, are certainly still among us. The Nobel laureate Francis Crick is one. Responding to the University of Pennsylvania SPECT-scan experiment on Buddhist monks, which showed that meditation resulted in notable changes in brain activity, Crick said, "A religious person would say there is no way you can explain what they experience in terms of what goes on inside their brain, that it must be their soul. I think that is an open question."[1] In his writings on the biology of consciousness, Crick argues that since the evidence leads one to believe that such an experience takes place in the brain, it cannot therefore be of the soul. Spirituality, in other words, has been explained away.

Steven Pinker, the renowned MIT neuroscientist, is another medical materialist. Human beings, he writes in *How the Mind Works*, "are organisms, not angels, and our minds are organs, not pipelines to truth." Our brains are not wired for the purpose of communing with nonearthly entities and perceiving the universe as an All, but "evolved by natural selection to solve problems that were life-and-death matters to our ancestors."[2] "Problem solving" is the all-purpose tool the brain developed in its Darwinian struggle to survive; religion is basically a massive misapplication of that tool to areas that are outside the brain's natural field.

This argument, spelled out by Pinker in 1997, is not new; it confronted William James in 1897, and it is basically a refurbishing of Freud's science-over-religion stance of half a century earlier: "Religion is an attempt to get control over the sensory world, in which we are placed, by means of the wish-world, which we have developed inside us as a result of biological and psychological necessities. But it cannot achieve its end. Its doctrines carry with them the stamp of the times in which they originated, the ignorant childhood days of the human race."[3]

One counter to the evolution argument, which has been put forth in a variety of ways, is that in fact evolution and spirituality are quite compatible. One could look at the evidence for the existence of religion in every known human society throughout history as supporting the theory that the ability of humans to transcend individual identity and unite with something larger has been partly responsible for the stability and success of the species. One could point to the many studies exploring the physiology of religious experience, which seem to show that prayer, meditation, and even simple church attendance have positive affects on rates of coronary disease, emphysema, blood pressure, myocardial infarction, cancer mortality, emphysema, and suicide. Such findings could further support the notion that religion is a function of evolution, for surely anything associated with better health is a boon to the species.

Still, the point of view that Crick and Pinker inhabit is powerful and pervasive. It is what causes us to feel, deep down, that this whole business of psychology venturing into religion and spirituality isn't quite right—the terrain is just too squishy for a would-be science.

This position seems valid and potentially unbeatable to us because most of us have a nineteenth-century scientist inside us. Reality, we believe (or believe that we are supposed to believe), comprises atoms and other tiny particles, which band together to make planets and trees and snakes: physical systems. Brains are also physical systems, which happen to have evolved to the point where we think, emote, and have self-consciousness. "Mind" and "soul," and their constituent parts (love, desire, annoyance, ecstasy, degradation, perkiness) can all be reduced to molecules at play. The predominance of this belief is directly related to the rise in popularity of medical treatments in psychology and psychiatry, and the decline in popularity in recent years of psychotherapy as a cure for serious mental illness—to the "quit the talk, just give me the Prozac" school of thought.

But those who argue in this way leave something out of their view of reality: us. The medical materialist (or scientific reductionist or classical scientist) likes to think that reality is out there going about its business, and that we just happen to have brains, which allow us to see reality, but that if we and our brains weren't here the atoms and molecules and planets and trees would go on doing what they do. In fact, people working today in neuroscience, psychology, and philosophy all converge on a very different point: that the perceiver is a still largely mysterious but undeniable participant in the reality he or she perceives. "Human consciousness," writes psychiatrist David Mann, "arises from the confrontation of subject and object."[4] Mann does not define consciousness as a subject that is bombarded by objects, but suggests that consciousness, in some way or other, *is* the subject-object dance. The world is an active participant in consciousness—it is a partner in it. Consciousness is both subject and object; it is perhaps largely as a matter of convenience that we metaphorically adopt the position of subject in some cases ("I shall now slap you"), object in others ("You slapped me!"), and, in still others, of objectifying third party ("Can you believe he slapped me?").

Paralleling the rise of the psyche-spirit movement in the 1990s was the rapidly coalescing field of consciousness studies, which has spawned interdisciplinary programs at dozens of universities involving fields as diverse as psychology, artificial intelligence, and quantum theory. These parallel developments are related. Both consciousness studies and the psyche-spirit movement have come about due to widespread feelings that the conventional understandings of what a human being is, how a human being knows, and what constitutes knowledge are inadequate and need a fairly drastic overhaul. In other words, both are due to the collapse of Cartesian dualism. Both implicitly assume that individual consciousness is broader, weirder, fuzzier than we normally allow, that it somehow or other extends beyond the skin of the individual person. Both represent the toppling of traditional boundaries that were erected in the classical period of science, and both bristle with debates about what the new model of consciousness ought to contain and where its boundaries should go.

These two movements encompass the various ways that people in several disciplines are taking up William James's challenge to bring individual consciousness into the sphere of science. There is, however, an inherent difficulty in doing this. One of the basic features of anybody's idea of a self is its subjectivity. A self knows it is a self, and with that knowing comes the whole feeling of "being oneself." This is what neuroscience calls "the hard problem" of consciousness: How can science, which is objective, analyzing things from the outside, possibly locate subjectivity? Even talking about the hard problem is hard, in part because the issue is almost too obvious. The philosopher Thomas Nagel best stated the problem in the influential 1974 essay "What Is It Like to Be a Bat?" The hard problem of consciousness, he said, is hard because while we can, from the objective stance, study a bat and understand how it navigates, respires, defecates, and reproduces, how its brain processes information, and how it makes decisions, and can make a thousand other more refined observations, we will still never, from this outside perspective, understand what it is like to be a bat. We can't get inside its skin. In a phrase that has been worked over by philosophers and psychologists in the years since the essay appeared, Nagel wrote that "the fact that an organism has conscious experience *at all* means, basically, that there is something it is like to *be* that organism."[5]

"Something it is like to be" is a philosopher's way of referring to individual awareness. Think of someone you believe you know well, then try to imagine that person from the inside: you quickly realize your knowledge of that person is quite fantastically small. You simply don't have a clue about his or her innermost hum of thoughts and feelings and prejudices, bitches and twitches and secret pleasures. You don't know how chocolate tastes to Fidel Castro or how the sand feels between Oprah Winfrey's toes. For that matter, you don't know what flying feels like to a bat, or how zebra tastes to a lion, or how a Led Zeppelin tune ("Stairway to Heaven," perhaps) strikes your infant son. Partly this inevitable unbridgable truth about reality, this preordained loneliness, explains the pull of sex, the need to merge with another, if only for a moment. And it accounts for the existence of novels and movies: for minutes at a time we try to slot ourselves into another subjectivity. They are a form of release, like all our hobbies and obsessions, another escape from the tomb of the self—only this time we escape into another self. We do it because in the crossing we experience a delight, a wash of freedom; somewhere in transit between ordinary self and fictional self we try on the experience of no self. This is why people talk about art as being another manifestation of religion. There is no church, but there is transcendence. Fiction is another holy drug.

Nagel leads the antireductionist brigade in the consciousness battle. We ought not, these people argue, allow ourselves to be convinced by medical materialists that if everything is matter then a spiritual understanding of reality is meaningless. Crick, Pinker, and the rest make a logical error: they equate objective knowing with knowing. The objective, scientific view of reality is what Nagel calls it in the title of one of his books, *The View from Nowhere*—that is, from no one's perspective. Objectivity, he reminds us (and it seems a strange statement at first), is not reality but only "a method of understanding." True, there is "a connection between objectivity and reality" but "not all reality is better understood the more objectively it is viewed."[6] Specifically, the material reductionists conveniently overlook the reality of their own consciousness, with its lush privacy and its howling imperfections. Or, to repeat William James's objection to this position:

> [I]t is absurd for science to say that the egotistic ele-
> ments of experience should be suppressed. The axis of
> reality runs solely through the egotistic places—they are
> strung upon it like so many beads. To describe the world
> with all its various feelings of the individual pinch of
> destiny, all the various spiritual attitudes, left out from
> the description—they being as describable as anything
> else—would be something like offering a printed bill of
> fare as the equivalent for a solid meal.[7]

The challenge, then, the ultimate goal, would be to create an approach to knowledge that embodies the subjective as well as the objective pole of experience. This is precisely what the psyche-spirit movement tries to do. It hopes to continue to expand the objective parameters of laboratory psychology—the ongoing refinement and sophistication of tools for the advancement of knowledge in neurology, behavioral psychology, and medicine—while also encouraging practitioners to swim with patients in the turbid waves of subjectivity, to inhabit the mystery in which the individualized grasp of reality is also, ironically, the road to its transcendence.

Whether it succeeds in achieving this goal depends on

whom you ask. If someone insists that science is by definition something that goes on outside the individual self, then the whole psyche-spirit business is a nonsensical waste of time. But if you care to believe that the self, the individual consciousness, is an active player in reality, then the universe of possibilities expands dramatically, for as everyone seems to agree, consciousness is a vast, strange, multilayered entity of which ordinary waking consciousness is only a sliver. As James famously put it:

> [O]ur normal waking consciousness, rational consciousness as we call it, is but one special type of consciousness, whilst all about it, parted from it by the filmiest of screens, there lie potential forms of consciousness entirely different. We may go through life without suspecting their existence; but apply the requisite stimulus, and at a touch they are there in all their completeness, definite types of mentality which probably somewhere have their field of application and adaptation. No account of the universe in its totality can be final which leaves these other forms of consciousness quite disregarded.[8]

The question posed a couple of chapters back was: Is there any scientific evidence to support the movement of psychiatry and psychology into the realm of the spirit? The answer seems to be yes. There is ample physical evidence, in brain and blood and breath, in cardiograms and cancer remission rates. Probably none of this evidence helps to weigh the claims of various psyche-spirit factions—deciding on the absolutist claims of Christian counselors or the extrasensory claims of alien abductionists remains as tricky as ever. The laboratory evidence does, however, further the cause of bringing spiritual experience into the zone of science—it gives a backbone of legitimacy to the psyche-spirit movement.

Ironically, this very evidence seems at first to erase the spiritual sphere; it seems to suggest that the whole business of religion is basically a magic show, a trick we play on ourselves. But that argument only holds if we treat objectivity and reality as one and the same; if we allow room for our own consciousness, then the sky is indeed the limit, for consciousness is the portal not only to the physical universe of classical science but to every other universe as well, including the universe of the spirit.

13

Beer, Sex, Shopping, Chocolate, God

We now spend a good deal more on drink and smoke than we spend on education. This, of course, is not surprising. The urge to escape from selfhood and the environment is in almost every- one almost all the time.

—ALDOUS HUXLEY

Ellen lives in New Jersey. She telephoned one day to say that "the men are back—the little men." They have vis- ited her before, hundreds of tiny bearded men in robes. They sit in a row along the top of the lacy shade over her bed- room window, reading books and praying. They are prophets, and they are praying for her. She is frightened of them because she knows other people do not have such visitors, but she fig- ures they are better than the others who come, the crocodile men she associates with evil, who, when she is going through a bad phase, fill her apartment to overflowing, so that she can hardly move around.

Adam lives with his parents on Long Island. He moved in with them after he "woke up" one day in 1994. The awakening was so violent it burned out much of his nervous system, so that today he has only limited control over his body. He now spends most of his day communing with the White Brother- hood, a group of souls who are helping this world to evolve.

Dorothy lives in Manhattan, where she is in the midst of her third kundalini experience. During the second, in 1978, she lost her apartment because she had the idea that the new age had come and the landlords had given all the apartments to the tenants. She got a room in the Chelsea Hotel and spent the next eleven months there, going out only for food, and otherwise communing with the souls of people who had died.

All of these people—and Lord knows how many more like them are out there—have shunned psychiatrists, even though most know that they have some pretty serious problems. They have not encountered a David Lukoff, a Paul Duckro, or a Stacy Davids. In their experience, a psychiatrist is someone who, almost by definition, does not understand. They are all suffering, and all avoid the profession that is supposed to help them. They represent gaps in the still-prevailing mental health model. Practitioners who favor the emerging one, the psyche-spirit model, would seem to have plenty of marginalized people in extreme circumstances who need their attention.

At the other end of the spectrum, meanwhile, are the rest of us. We are their other great untapped client pool. One of the tenets of a psychospiritual perspective is that spirituality, striving for something beyond the confines of ordinary individual consciousness, is natural to us all. If the socially sanctioned paths to it—religions—are cut off or overgrown or otherwise useless, we find others. Madness is one alternate route. But there may be others. There may be paths that are not authorized by any known church or temple, and that also don't fit the definition of serious mental illness. These are the paths that crisscross the terrain of ordinary life, the ways that all of us, every day, try to break free.

Andre Papineau has a perspective on the confluence of psychology and spirituality that does not rely on brain scans or work with the seriously mentally ill, but on time spent, over the years, with ordinary people and their ordinary problems.

Papineau is a Catholic priest from Milwaukee, a steel-haired, portly but sprightly man with the voice of a 1940s radio announcer. As a clergyman who cofounded the Jung Center in Milwaukee, teaches pastoral studies, and travels the country lecturing on addiction, depression, and life transitions, Papineau is a crossover figure in the psyche-spirit movement, a switch-hitter. One might put him in the pastoral counseling category, except that he has never had a congregation to shepherd. He is a career educator, in seminaries and through the continuing education circuit. When people tell him their problems, he listens with both a cultivated understanding of the byways of human emotions and a sophisticated sense of spiritual longings. In Papineau's mind the currents of psyche and spirit flow together into one stream; to him the dozens of minor psychological agonies that we suffer from in our everyday lives are just as susceptible to a spiritual reading as the more exotic forms of mental illness.

Addiction is one of Papineau's favorite topics. Addiction, in his mind, is an intriguing, ornately carved, though tragically short flight on the staircase of psychospiritual transcendence. For an old-fashioned drunk, sitting of an afternoon in a dark, stale-smelling bar, Papineau will tell you, "God is in the beer." You might think that by this he means that the alcoholic worships his drink, and you would be right. But he means it truly, not ironically. Alcoholics are initiates into the Mystery, as true a group of seekers as those in any seminary or yeshiva. This is not, Papineau admits, a politically correct observation, but he believes it is a compelling one.

His starting point for this insight, which he developed over years of working with people who are struggling with the modest tortures of life, was Jung, who expressed to Bill W., the founder of Alcoholics Anonymous, his belief that "craving for alcohol was the equivalent, on a low level, of the spiritual thirst of our being for wholeness."[1] (William James too insisted that the "drunken consciousness is one bit of the mystic consciousness.")[2] The Jungian Self, the center of the psyche, the part of the individual that seeks union with the infinite, tries to achieve this union by projecting its internal striving outward, onto an object. In the case of an alcoholic, the object is drink.

To this psychological perspective Papineau adds a religious layer, borrowed from the Catholic theologian Karl Rahner. Rahner talked about what he called the transcendental horizon: the visible edge of wholeness and infinity toward which the soul continually journeys but never truly reaches. This horizon is the farthest, highest, and truest home of all our longings. It is the oxygen from which every human act of love and knowledge takes its breath.

Put simplistically, a psychological view locates the ultimate goal and source of this longing—the Self—inside the person, while some theological views call it God and place it on the outside. But in overcoming the dualistic split between body and mind/soul, one transcends the split between earth and heaven. If you come to see all reality as one, then religion and psychology merge, or at least significantly blend into one another. Psychological problems become spiritual problems, and are susceptible to spiritual solutions.

This awareness is not Papineau's alone. In varying degrees one might say it is shared by all psyche-spirit practitioners. Paul Duckro considers that a woman with an eating disorder may be acting out a spiritual hunger; Tomás Agosin sees a patient's falling in love with him as a projection of her Self, her "God-within," onto him. These interpretations come from the doctors' seeing body, mind, and soul as all of one substance, or on one continuum.

But Andre Papineau goes a bit further. What he is getting at in talking about addiction is, in part, the psychospiritual core of

Alcoholics Anonymous: You have sought spiritual fulfillment, but in the wrong place; now put yourself directly in God's hands. But, according to Papineau, the twelve-step programs highlight only part of the truth. The darker reality is that the alcoholic, drink in hand, *is* on a spiritual path—as is a heroin addict, a crackhead, even a chainsmoker. The spiritual component isn't the thing itself but the longing. In the reaching out for the object of mystery, the self vanishes; you become an arrow. "The point is that we are all drawn toward the transcendent, the Other," he said. "And that is, inevitably, an impossible goal to achieve. We reach out for It, capital I . . . but find that what we have grabbed is an it—a lowercase *thing*. So we supercharge this thing, this mere object. We invest it with transcendent energy."

Alcohol is one of the many objects that we supercharge. Addiction is a clinical term for a particular pitch this universal striving may take. Addictions, delights, interests, obsessions, preoccupations, tics, and hobbies: all are escapes from the self to the Self, all are roads to the transcendental horizon. It can be sought in beer, chocolate, cigarettes, gambling, shoes, antiques, old coins, garden gnomes, lacquer boxes, model trains, porcelain vases, elephant earrings, heirloom seeds, or baseball cards. It can be sought in overeating or dieting, in orgasms or old movies. Practically anything can trip the lock on the self and send it on the path of transcendence. One needn't be clinically addicted for it to happen—a DSM diagnosis is not a prerequisite to entering the psychospiritual sphere. Having a passion or hobby will do. Curiosity and arousal are just fine. To a genuine religious sensibility, everything is spiritual.

One difficulty with this view is that according to traditional psychology (and common sense) developing an intense passion for gambling or sex or vodka or chocolate is not a good at all but a defense, a weakness, an escape from reality. How can such strivings be that and also genuine spiritual endeavors? Perhaps because we live in the here and now: a spiritual journey may be a journey of psychological growth, but if it comes at the expense of ordinary concerns—of family, work, physical health—it is flawed, for in its passionate reaching it forgets what is right in front of us, which is at least half of what it means to be human.

In Andre Papineau's widened psychospiritual sensibility, the healthiest of strivings are, at least part of the way, indistinguishable from the vices and obsessions. To have, rear, and love children, to bond with friends and community, to give oneself, to live and die well: these are psychospiritual strivings, journeys toward the horizon. Love is the quintessential road to that horizon. Losing yourself in the mystery of another is the definition of love; head-over-heels is a state of intoxication. "In love," Papineau said, "you reach out for that transcendent horizon, and find it embodied in another person. But in supercharging this other, you place an impossible burden of expectation on the person. Eventually you realize the person isn't the All. You become disillusioned."

This is where things get interesting. Depression too is a psychospiritual condition. Disillusionment, Papineau believes, whether with a lover, a drug, or life, is "a form of liberation." The Latin root of illusion is *ludere*, to play. If all of our striving, transcendence-seeking activities—love affairs, pastimes, business ambitions—are destined to come up short of the ultimate, they are all illusive, but this fact does not mean that we should not reach outward (the only other choice is to reach inward—to sink into narcissism), but that we should keep the element of play alive in them. Play can be a serious thing, but it also has an aspect of lightness. We should proceed, but stay light on our feet. "Young people entering the work force often have the feeling that they are just playing at jobs," Papineau said. "They think, 'I'm just acting this role, and somebody's going to find me out.' They think there is something wrong with them. But I think they are just being honest. We are all only playing roles. When you start to take your role too seriously it becomes dangerous. We should be like an actor onstage. He knows he's playing, but at the same time he takes his role seriously. The disillusionment, so to speak, comes at the end of the play, when everyone lets the illusion drop."

To take the play too seriously is to forget that the object of your striving—love, success, God—is not the transcendent and universal reality but an echo of it. If addiction is a spiritual pursuit, the problem comes when it settles in. An alcoholic will tell you he both loves and hates his drink. The hate is a signal to lighten up, to move on. The trap in objectifying the search for mystery is that we come to take the object seriously.

Perhaps this is one of the more important lessons we can take from the opening-up of psychology into the realm of religion, and one that applies to all of us. It might be a useful way to understand what separates the psychotic and the mystic, as well as what distinguishes the addict or the obsessive from the comparatively free striver. The one is dead certain, serious as a heart attack, hanging on for dear life. The other has learned how to play.

Notes

1. THE NEW PSYCHOTICS

1. Harold Kaplan, Benjamin Sadock, and Jack Grebb, *Kaplan and Sadock's Synopsis of Psychiatry*, 7th ed. (Baltimore: Williams & Wilkins, 1994), pp. 819, 820, 1084.

2. R. D. Laing, "Transcendental Experience in Relation to Religion and Psychosis," in Stanislav Grof and Christina Grof, *Spiritual Emergency* (New York: Putnam's, 1989), pp. 53, 54.

3. John Foskett, "Christianity and Psychiatry," in *Psychiatry and Religion*, Dinesh Bhugra, ed., (London: Routledge, 1996), p. 56.

4. David Lukoff, "A Holistic Program for Chronic Schizophrenia Patients," *Schizophrenia Bulletin* 12, no. 2 (1986).

5. Allen Ginsberg, "Psalm IV," in *Selected Poems 1947–1995* (New York: HarperCollins, 1998).

6. Abraham Maslow, *Religions, Values, and Peak Experiences* (Cleveland: Ohio State University, 1964), pp. 59–68.

2. THE SINGULAR PLURALISM OF WILLIAM JAMES

1. Linda Simon, *Genuine Reality: A Life of William James* (New York: Harcourt, Brace, 1998), p. 247.

2. William James, *The Varieties of Religious Experience* (New York: Penguin, 1982), p. 499.

3. ———, *A Pluralistic Universe*, vol. 4 of *The Works of William James* (Cambridge: Harvard University Press, 1977), p. 282.

4. ———, *Essays in Philosophy*, vol. 5 of *The Works of William James* (Cambridge: Harvard University Press, 1977), p. 21.

5. L. A. Govinda, *Foundations of Tibetan Mysticism* (New York: Samuel Weiser, 1974), p. 93.

6. Werner Heisenberg, *Physics and Philosophy* (New York: Harper, 1958), p. 81.

7. James, *Varieties*, p. 132.

8. William James, *The Principles of Psychology* (Chicago: Encyclopaedia Britannica, 1980), pp. 118–19.

9. James, *Varieties*, pp. 13, 14.

10. Ibid., p. 10.

11. Ibid., p. 7.

12. Sigmund Freud, *Civilization and Its Discontents*, vol. 21 of *The Standard Edition of the Complete Psychological Works of Sigmund Freud* (London: Hogarth, 1961), p. 65.

13. Quoted in Martin Marty's Introduction to James, *Varieties*, p. xxiv.

14. James, *Pluralistic*, p. 139.

15. Carl Jung, *Memories, Dreams, Reflections* (New York: Random House, 1965), pp. 155–56.

16. ———, *Symbols of Transformation*, vol. 5 of *Collected Works* (Princeton: Bollingen, 1967), p. 137.

17. Jung, *Memories*, p. 156.

18. Quoted in Peter Gay, *A Godless Jew* (New Haven: Yale University Press, 1987), p. 18.

19. Quoted in Ibid., p. 48.

20. Sigmund Freud, *The Future of an Illusion* (New York: Norton, 1956), pp. 8, 9, 69, 70.

21. Frederick Crews, ed., *Unauthorized Freud* (New York: Viking, 1998), p. 126.

22. Harold Kaplan, Benjamin Sadock, and Jack Grebb, *Kaplan and Sadock's Synopsis of Psychiatry*, 7th ed. (Baltimore: Williams & Wilkins, 1994), pp. 135–39.

3. ZEITGEIST

1. Quoted in Peter Gay, *A Godless Jew* (New Haven: Yale University Press, 1987), p. 76.

2. Quoted in Ibid., p. 75.

3. Quoted in Ibid., p. 82.

4. Quoted in Ibid., p. 83.

5. Paul Fleischman, *The Healing Spirit* (New York: Paragon House, 1989), p. 26.

6. Ibid., pp. 173–74.

7. Patanjali, *How to Know God: The Yoga Aphorisms of Patanjali*, trans. and commentary by Swami Prabhavananda and Christopher Isherwood (New York: New American Library, 1969), p. 114.

8. Fleischman, *Healing*, p. 174.

9. Ibid., p. 175.

10. Ibid., p. 116.

11. Paul Fleischman, *Spiritual Aspects of Psychiatric Practice* (Cleveland, S.C.: Bonne Chance Press, 1993), p. 33.

12. Ibid., p. 34.

13. Ibid., p. 32.

14. Ibid., p. 33.

4. STORMING THE CASTLE

1. Ernest Jones, *The Life and Work of Sigmund Freud* (Garden City, N.Y.: Anchor Books, 1963), p. 455.
2. Group for the Advancement of Psychiatry, *Mysticism: Spiritual Quest or Mental Disorder* (New York: Group for the Advancement of Psychiatry, 1976).
3. Tomás Agosin, "Psychosis, Dreams, and Mysticism in the Clinical Domain," in *The Fires of Desire*, F. R. Halligan and J. J. Shea, eds. (New York: Crossroad, 1992), p. 44.
4. Ibid., pp. 42–43.
5. Quotes regarding this and the following patient are from ibid., pp. 46–61.
6. John 6:53–57.
7. Erich Fromm, "Psychoanalysis and Zen Buddhism," in D. T. Suzuki, Erich Fromm, and Richard De Martino, *Zen Buddhism and Psychoanalysis* (New York: Grove, 1963), p. 78.
8. Erich Fromm, *The Art of Loving* (New York: Harper, 1956), p. 45.
9. Ibid., p. 55.
10. Erich Fromm, *Psychoanalysis and Religion* (New Haven: Yale University Press, 1967), p. 37.
11. Ibid., p. 37.
12. Ibid., p. viii.
13. Fromm, "Psychoanalysis and Zen Buddhism," p. 122.
14. Jeffrey Levin, David Larson, and Christina Puchalski, "Religion and Spirituality in Medicine: Research and Education," in *Journal of the American Medical Association* (3) September 1997: 792.
15. David Larson, James Swyers, and Michael McCullough, eds., *Scientific Research on Spirituality and Health: A Consensus Report* (Rockville, Md.: National Institute for Healthcare Research, 1997), p. 8.
16. William James, *The Varieties of Religious Experience* (New York: Penguin, 1982), p. 458.

5. THE DON QUIXOTE OF WESTCHESTER

1. Miguel de Cervantes, *The History of Don Quixote de la Mancha*, trans. John Ormsby (Chicago: Encyclopaedia Britannica, 1980), p. 2.
2. Martin Buber, *The Knowledge of Man*, trans. M. Friedman and R. G. Smith (New York: Harper & Row, 1965), p. 74.
3. Ibid., p. 74.

6. AT THE CENTER FOR THE SPIRITUALLY DISTURBED

1. Paul Duckro, John Chibnall, and Ann Wolf, "Women's Religious and Sexual Trauma," in *Review for Religious* (1998): 307.
2. Mark 5:1–13.
3. John Dominic Crossan, *The Historical Jesus* (San Francisco, Harper San Francisco, 1991), pp. 314–18.
4. American Psychiatric Association, *Diagnostic and Statistical Manual of Mental*

Disorders, Fourth Edition (Washington, D.C.: American Psychiatric Association, 1994), p. 533.

5. Harold Kaplan, Benjamin Sadock, and Jack Grebb, *Kaplan and Sadock's Synopsis of Psychiatry*, 7th ed. (Baltimore: Williams & Wilkins, 1994), p. 621.

6. Stevan Davies, *Jesus the Healer* (New York: Continuum, 1995), p. 73.

7. Ibid., p. 75.

8. Mark 2:11–12.

7. THE PATIENTS OF JOB

1. Job 3:11–13.

8. CRUSADERS

1. Elizabeth Mehren, "Killer of 2 at Abortion Clinics Commits Suicide," *Los Angeles Times*, 30 November 1996, p. A24.

2. Associated Press, "Priest Predicts Killing of Abortion-Rights Supporters," 20 July 1994.

3. Eric Wee, "Abortion Opponents," *Washington Post*, 2 January 1995, p. A6.

4. Frederick Hacker, *Crusaders, Criminals, Crazies: Terror and Terrorism in Our Time* (New York: Norton, 1976), p. 70.

5. Psalm 143.

6. Paul Fleischman, *The Healing Spirit* (New York: Paragon House, 1989), p. 8.

7. Ibid., p. 10.

8. This and the following quotes are taken from the transcript of Salvi's competency hearing, Commonwealth of Massachusetts, Norfolk, Superior Court, no. 9518–24, *Commonwealth* v. *John Salvi*, Dedham, Massachusetts, July 24, 1994.

9. Robert Coles, *The Mind's Fate* (Boston: Little, Brown, 1995), p. 291.

10. Robert Funk, "God and the Emperor at Waco," *The Fourth R*, May/June 1993, 16.

11. Hacker, *Crusaders*, p. 83.

12. From the psychiatric interview for Salvi's competency hearing, January 15, 1995.

9. THE WALKING SYMBOL

1. Quoted in Maurice Friedman, *Religion and Psychology* (New York: Paragon House, 1992), p. 182.

2. Ibid., p. 180.

3. Anton Boisen, *The Exploration of the Inner World* (Philadelphia: Harper & Row, 1945), p. 5.

4. John Foskett, "Christianity and Psychiatry," in *Psychiatry and Religion*, Dinesh Bhugra, ed. (London: Routledge, 1996), p. 59.

5. Robert Coles, *The Mind's Fate* (Boston: Little, Brown, 1995), p. 114.

6. Boisen, *Exploration*, p. 192–93.

7. Timothy Carson, *Liminal Reality and Transformational Power* (Lanham, Md.: University Press of America, 1997), manuscript, p. 24.

8. Otto Billig, et al., "Schizophrenic Graphic Expression and Tribal Art in New

Guinea," in *Anthropology and Mental Health*, Joseph Westermeyer, ed. (The Hague: Mouton, 1976).

9. Quoted in Bhugra, *Psychiatry and Religion*, p. 217.

10. William James, *The Varieties of Religious Experience* (New York: Penguin, 1982), p. 464.

11. Mother Teresa, *Everything Starts from Prayer*, Anthony Stern ed., (Ashland, Ore.: White Cloud, 1998), p. 50.

12. Stifler, Greer, Sneck, and Dovenmuehle, "An Empirical Investigation of the Discriminability of Reported Mystical Experiences Among Religious Contemplatives, Psychotic Inpatients, and Normal Adults," in *Journal for the Scientific Study of Religion*, 1 December 1993.

13. Quoted in Ruth Anna Putnam, ed., *The Cambridge Companion to William James* (Cambridge: Cambridge University Press, 1997), p. 229.

10. SATAN IN THE BRAIN

1. Joseph Nicolosi, "Can Male Homosexuals Be Helped to Change?" *Christian Counseling Today* 5, no. 1, (1997): 11.

2. Stephen Arterburn, "What Makes Christian Counseling Christian?" *Ministries Today*, November/December 1995, p. 7.

3. Ibid.

4. John Mack, *Abduction* (New York: Scribner's, 1994), pp. 407–8.

5. John Steinbeck, *East of Eden* (New York: Penguin, 1992), p. 72.

6. Daniel Dennett, *Consciousness Explained* (Boston: Little, Brown, 1991), p. 35.

7. Dinesh Bhugra, ed., *Psychiatry and Religion* (London: Routledge, 1996), p. 173.

8. Robert Lee Hotz, "Brain Could Affect Religious Response, Researchers Report," *Los Angeles Times*, 1 November 1997, p. B4.

9. David Larson, James Swyers, and Michael McCullough, eds., *Scientific Research on Spirituality and Health: A Consensus Report* (Rockville, Md.: National Institute for Healthcare Research, 1997), p. 90.

10. Marilyn Schlitz, "Healing Effects of Intercessory Prayer and Distant Intentionality," paper delivered to Spirituality and Healing in Medicine II, Boston, December 15–17, 1996.

11. ACID FLASHBACK

1. Albert Hofmann, *LSD: My Problem Child* (New York: McGraw-Hill, 1980), p. 5.

2. Richard Yensen, and Donna Dryer, "Thirty Years of Psychedelic Research: The Spring Grove Experiment and Its Sequels," in A. Dittrich, A. Hofmann, and H. Leuner, *Welten des Bewusstseins*, bd. 4, Bedeutung für die Psychotherapie; VWB Berlin, 1994, p. 74.

3. Ibid., p. 75.

4. Walter Pahnke, "Drugs and Mysticism," in *The International Journal of Parapsychology* 8, no. 2 (Spring 1966): 295.

5. Quoted in Rick Doblin, "Pahnke's 'Good Friday Experiment': A Long-Term Follow-Up and Methodological Critique," *Journal of Transpersonal Psychology* 23, no. 1 (1991): 13.

6. William James, *The Varieties of Religious Experience* (New York: Penguin, 1982), pp. 387–88.

7. Doblin, "Pahnke's," p. 12.

8. M. Spitzer, et al., "Increased Activation of Indirect Semantic Associations Under Psilocybin," *Biological Psychiatry* 39:1055; reported in Matthew Baggott, "Psilocybin's Effects on Cognition," *Multidisciplinary Association for Psychedelic Studies*, (Winter 1996/97): 10.

9. Rev. Mike Young, "If I Could Change Your Mind," sermon of November 5, 1995, First Unitarian Church of Honolulu.

10. Huston Smith, "Do Drugs Have Religious Import?" *Journal of Philosophy*, 17 September 1964.

11. David Larson, James Swyers, and Michael McCullough, eds., *Scientific Research on Spirituality and Health: A Consensus Report* (Rockville, Md.: National Institute for Healthcare Research, 1997), p. 90.

12. EXPERIENCE ITSELF

1. Francis Crick, quoted in "Seeking the Biology of Spirituality," *Los Angeles Times*, 26 April 1998, p. A-1.

2. Steven Pinker, *How the Mind Works* (New York: Norton, 1997).

3. Sigmund Freud, *New Introductory Lectures on Psycho-Analysis*, trans. J. H. Sprott, (New York: Norton, 1933), pp. 217–20.

4. David Mann, *A Simple Theory of the Self* (New York: Norton, 1994), p. 5.

5. Thomas Nagel, "What Is It Like to Be a Bat?" in *Philosophical Review*, 1974; reprinted in *Mortal Questions* (Cambridge: Cambridge University Press, 1991).

6. ———, *The View from Nowhere* (New York: Oxford University Press, 1986), p. 4.

7. William James, *The Varieties of Religious Experience* (New York: Penguin, 1982), p. 499.

8. Ibid., p. 388.

13. BEER, SEX, SHOPPING, CHOCOLATE, GOD

1. Carl Jung, "The Bill W.–Carl Jung Letters," *ReVision* 10, no. 2: 20.

2. William James, *The Varieties of Religious Experience* (New York: Penguin, 1982), p. 387.

Index